A Manual of Percussion and Auscultation

Austin Flint

Contents

PREFACE. 7
MANUAL OF PERCUSSION AND AUSCULTATION. 8
CHAPTER I. INTRODUCTION. 8
CHAPTER II. PERCUSSION IN HEALTH. 27
CHAPTER III. PERCUSSION IN DISEASE. 39
CHAPTER IV. AUSCULTATION IN HEALTH. 46
CHAPTER V. AUSCULTATION IN DISEASE. 60
CHAPTER VI. THE PHYSICAL DIAGNOSIS ....
      OF DISEASES OF THE RESPIRATORY SYSTEM. 93
CHAPTER VII. THE PHYSICAL CONDITIONS ....
      OF THE HEART IN HEALTH AND DISEASE. 124
CHAPTER VIII THE PHYSICAL DIAGNOSIS OF ....
      DISEASES OF THE HEART AND OF THORACIC ANEURISM. 148

A MANUAL OF PERCUSSION AND AUSCULTATION

BY

Austin Flint

PREFACE.

THIS work contains the substance of the lessons which the author has for many years given, in connection with practical instruction in percussion and auscultation, to private classes composed of medical students and practitioners.

In his courses of practical instruction, his plan has been, 1st. To simplify the subject as much as possible, avoiding all needless refinements; 2nd. To consider the distinctive characters of the different physical signs as determined, not by analogies, nor by deductions from physics, but by analysis, and as based especially on variations in the intensity, pitch, and quality of sounds; 3rd. To impress the fact that the significance of physical signs relates to certain physical conditions, and the importance of a familiar acquaintance with these conditions, as well as with the distinctive characters of the signs by which they are represented; 4th. To enforce the necessity of sufficient study of the physical conditions and the signs of health, as a ***sine qua non*** for success in the study of the physical diagnosis of diseases; and, 5th. To waive discussion of the mechanism of signs, whenever this is open for discussion, taking the ground that our knowledge of the significance of signs rests solely on the constancy of their connection with the physical conditions which they represent.

This plan has been pursued in writing the book, which the author hopes may be found useful, not only to medical students engaged in the practical study of percussion and auscultation, but, as a handbook for reference, to the practitioner of medicine.

NEW YORK, June, 1876.

MANUAL OF PERCUSSION AND AUSCULTATION.

CHAPTER I.

INTRODUCTION.

Definition of percussion and auscultation—The sounds obtained by these methods representing healthy and morbid physical conditions—Definition of signs—The basis of our knowledge of signs the constancy of association of certain sounds with certain physical conditions in health and disease—The present state of perfection of our knowledge of signs furnished by percussion and auscultation—Requirements for the successful study of these methods of exploration—The anatomy and physiology of the chest—An enumeration of the points relating thereto which are of especial importance—The physical conditions incident to the different diseases of the chest: the conditions relating to the respiratory system stated, and a summary of them—The distinctive characters of healthy and morbid signs; variations in intensity, pitch, and quality, considered as the chief source of the characters distinguishing the signs of disease from each other and from those of health—Other distinctions than those of intensity, pitch, and quality—The analytical method of the study of percussion and auscultation—The significance of the signs as regards the physical conditions which they severally represent—Morbid conditions, not individual diseases, represented by the morbid signs—Regional divisions of the chest—Anatomical relations of the regions severally to the parts within the chest.

Physical Exploration.

THE physical exploration of the chest embraces six different methods, namely: percussion, auscultation, inspection, palpation, mensuration, and succussion. Of these, percussion and auscultation, dealing with sounds, involve the sense of hearing. In percussion, the sounds are produced by striking upon the walls of the chest; in auscultation, they are caused by acts of breathing, speaking, and coughing.

The sounds in percussion and auscultation are, 1st, normal or healthy sounds, being produced when there is no disease of the chest; and, 2nd, abnormal or morbid sounds, being produced when the chest is the seat of disease. The sounds, healthy and morbid, constitute what are known as physical signs. Frequently, for the sake of brevity, the term signs, without the word physical, is used to denote these sounds. Conventionally, physical signs, or signs, are terms employed in a sense of contradistinction from the term symptoms. The signs are distinguished, of course, as normal or healthy and abnormal or morbid.

The sounds which constitute signs represent certain physical conditions pertaining to the chest. The normal or healthy signs represent physical conditions existing when the organs are not affected by disease; the abnormal or morbid signs represent physical conditions which are deviations from those of health, being incident to the various diseases of the chest. The physical conditions represented by signs may be distinguished as normal or healthy, and abnormal or morbid conditions.

The representation of healthy and morbid physical conditions by certain healthy and morbid signs is established by having ascertained a constancy of association of the signs with the conditions. This constancy of association is ascertained by observation or experience. The sounds which are constantly obtained by percussion and auscultation in health are thereby established signs of healthy conditions, and the sounds which are only obtained in cases of disease are thereby established signs of morbid conditions. Our knowledge of certain sounds as the signs of certain physical conditions can have no reliable basis other than the constancy of the connection of the former with the latter. This constancy of connection is determined by the study of the sounds during life and examination of the organs after death. The existence of certain conditions is not to be inferred from the characters of certain sounds until the connection of the sounds with the conditions has been ascertained by experience; then, and then only, are the sounds to be reckoned as signs of these conditions. So, also, it is not to be inferred from certain physical conditions found after death, that certain sounds must have been produced during life, until the connection between the conditions and the sounds has been ascertained by experience. In other words, our knowledge of signs as representing physical conditions, can rest on no other than a purely empirical foundation.

Our knowledge of the signs representing the physical conditions in health and disease, thanks to the labors of Laennec and of those who have followed in his footsteps, has been brought to great perfection. The practical object of this knowledge is to determine by means of percussion and auscultation, together with the other methods of exploration, the existence of either healthy or morbid physical conditions, and to discriminate the latter from each other; that is to say, the practical object is diagnosis. The signs now known to represent physical conditions, healthy and morbid, taken in connection with symptoms and pathological laws, render, for the most part, the diagnosis of diseases of the chest easy and positive. Hence, it becomes the duty of the medical student and practitioner to give to percussion and auscultation attention sufficient, at least, for their practical application to the diagnosis of the diseases commonly met with in medical practice; and this duty is the more imperative because it involves neither peculiar difficulties nor great labor. In entering upon the undertaking, it is important to consider the requirements for the successful study of this province of practical medicine. These requirements relate to: 1st, the anatomy and physiology of the chest; 2nd, the morbid physical conditions incident to the different diseases of the chest; 3rd, the distinctive characters of healthy and morbid signs; and 4th, the significance of the signs as regards the physical conditions which they severally represent.

Anatomy and Physiology of the Chest.

The necessity of a certain amount of knowledge of the anatomy and physiology of the chest, as a requirement for the study of percussion and auscultation, together with the other methods of physical exploration, is too obvious to need any discussion. The physical conditions of health must be known as preparatory for appreciating the physical conditions of disease. It would be absurd to think of studying the latter until the former are known. The student, therefore, who is not acquainted with the anatomy and physiology of the chest, must defer entering upon the study of physical diagnosis until this requirement is fulfilled. Familiarity with the morbid physical conditions is necessary; and for the advanced medical student or the practitioner, it is advisable to refresh the memory with a review of certain anatomical and physiological points before beginning the study of percussion and auscultation. These points, relating especially to the physical conditions of health, cannot be considered in this work. A simple enumeration of them can only be introduced, the reader being referred for details to treatises on anatomy and physiology.

Important anatomical conditions relate to the bones of the cheat, namely, the general conformation of the thorax; the differences in respect of the obliquity of the ribs, from above downward; the direction of the costal cartilages, their connection with the sternum, and the angles formed by the junction of the ribs and cartilages; the differences in width of the intercostal spaces in the upper, middle, and lower portions of the anterior, lateral, and posterior aspects of the thorax, together with the relations of the scapula and clavicle. The relative thickness of the muscular covering of the chest in different situations is to be considered, and, in women, the varying size of the mammæ. The attachments of the diaphragm to the thoracic walls, and its relations to the organs below, as well as above it, are points of importance.

Important physiological conditions relate to the parts which the ribs, costal cartilages, sternum, and diaphragm severally play in the movements of respiration. The differences, in respect of these movements, in tranquil and in forced breathing; the contrast between the two sexes, and between early and advanced life are points to be studied. Other points are, the frequency of the respiration in health, and the relative duration, rapidity, and force of the inspiratory and the expiratory movements.

Numerous anatomical and physiological points pertain to the organs within the chest. The more important of these, relating to normal physical conditions, are the following: 1st, as regards the lungs, the connections of the pleura, and the smoothness of the pleural surfaces in contact with each other; the relations of the apex and base of each lung to the chest-walls, and the differences of the two lungs in this respect; the relative spaces occupied respectively by the two lobes of the left, and the three lobes of the right, lung; the situation of the interlobar fissures in either side on the posterior, lateral, and anterior aspects of the chest; the arrangement of the air vesicles, pulmonary lobules, and the different sized infra-pulmonary bronchial tubes; the expansion of the air vesicles, and the movement of the current of air from larger to smaller bronchial tubes in the act of inspiration, the vesicles diminishing in size, and the current of air moving from smaller to larger tubes in the act of expiration; the difference in respect of the relative proportion of air and solids at the end of inspiration and at the end of expiration; the extent to which the volume of the lungs may be diminished by a forced act of expiration, and increased by a forced act of inspiration; the relations of the apices to the subclavian arteries, and the variable extent to which the apex rises on either side above the clavicle. 2d, as regards the larynx, trachea, and the bronchial tubes without the lungs, the anatomy and physiology of the vocal chords, of the muscles concerned in the movements of respiration and of phonation, with the relations of each to the recurrent laryngeal nerve; the size of the rima glottidis in youth, after puberty, and relatively in the two sexes; the difference in the amount of areolar tissue above the vocal chords in children and in adults; the situation of the trachea, and the point of its bifurcation; the length, direction, and size of the two primary bronchi contrasted with each other, and the secondary branches which penetrate the lungs. 3d, as regards the heart, the boundaries of the space which it occupies—that is, of the præcordial space; the relations of the aorta and pulmonic artery to the walls of the chest, the portions of the præcordial space in which the heart is covered and uncovered by lung; the situations of the auricles and ventricles respectively; the relations of these to each other, and the arrangements of the valves; the currents of blood through the orifices within the heart, and the relations of each of these to the heart-sounds; the rhythmical succession of these sounds, and the differences which distinguish each from the other in respect of loudness, duration, tone, quality, extent of diffusion, and the situation in which each has its maximum of intensity; the mechanism of these sounds, and the situation of the apex-beat.

The foregoing are the anatomical and physiological points which especially claim attention with reference to normal physical conditions preparatory to entering on the study of abnormal physical conditions represented by the signs famished by percussion and auscultation, together with the other methods of physical exploration.

The Physical Conditions Incident to the Different Diseases of the Respiratory System.

The numerous physical conditions incident to different diseases must be known, for it is the immediate object of percussion, auscultation, and the other methods of exploration, to ascertain either the existence or the absence of these conditions. Knowledge of all the important conditions which are deviations from those of health, and the relations of each to different diseases, is, therefore, an essential requirement.

Deviations from the normal conformation of the chest, and the various abnormal movements of respiration, belong properly among the physical signs obtained by inspection, palpation, and mensuration. For the most part, these signs represent morbid physical conditions within the chest. Certain conditions relating to the pleura are accumulations of liquid, serous or purulent, within the pleural sac. The quantity of liquid may be large enough to compress the lung into a solid mass, and to enlarge the affected side, at the same time restraining or annulling the respiratory movements; the chest on the affected side, then, will contain only lung solidified by compression and liquid. In other cases the quantity of liquid is either small, moderate, or considerable, the lung, then, containing a lessened quantity of air, and its volume diminished in proportion to the amount of liquid. These conditions are incident to simple pleurisy with effusion, pyothorax or empyema, and hydrothorax.

The pleural surfaces, in cases of pleurisy, may be more or less covered with recent lymph, and, when not separated by the presence of liquid, they do not move upon each other smoothly and noiselessly. The friction of the opposed surfaces is still more productive of audible and sometimes tactile signs after the absorption of liquid, when the exuded lymph has become more adherent and dense than when it is recent.

The presence of air in the pleural space, either alone or with more or less liquid, in pneumothorax, may compress the lung into a solid mass, also dilating the affected side, and restraining or annulling its movements; and the air, with or without liquid, when not in sufficient quantity to produce these effects, may diminish more or less the volume of the lung and the amount of air in the pulmonary vesicles. These conditions give rise to characteristic physical signs. The perforation of lung, usually existing in cases of pneumothorax, occasions additional signs which are characteristic.

Solidification of lung is an important physical condition incident to several diseases, irrespective of the condensation just referred to caused by the compression of liquid or air in the pleural sac. Complete consolidation of an entire lobe, or of two and even three lobes, exists in the second stage of lobar pneumonia. Certain physical signs are found to represent this condition of complete solidification. The different degrees of solidification, namely, slight, moderate, and considerable, occur during the stage of resolution in cases of pneumonia, and these gradations are severally represented by well-defined characters pertaining to physical signs. Solidification, circumscribed, forming nodules which vary in degree and in the extent of lung affected, occurring either in one situation or more or less numerous, situated in the upper, lower, or middle portion of the lung, either on one side or on both sides, exists in phthisis, in broncho-pneumonia or collapse of pulmonary lobules, in hydatids, in hemorrhagic infarct us or embolic pneumonia, in pulmonary gangrene, and in carcinoma. It exists, greater or less in degree and more or less extended, in interstitial pneumonia. In these different connections the existence of solidification, its degree and extent, its limitation to one situation or its existence at different points, are determinable by means of physical signs.

A physical condition the opposite of solidification is an abnormal accumulation of air within the air vesicles of the lungs. This is incident to pulmonary or vesicular emphysema, arising from a morbid dilatation of the air vesicles. The permanent expansion and increased volume of the upper lobes in some cases of this disease, occasion a characteristic deformity of the chest, together with certain deviations from the normal movements of respiration, which are also characteristic. This condition is represented by distinctive signs furnished by percussion and auscultation. Interstitial emphysema, that is, the extravasation of air in the areolar tissue, or interlobular emphysema, in like manner gives rise to signs furnished by these methods of exploration.

The presence of a viscid exudation within the air vesicles and bronchioles, is a morbid physical condition incident to vesicular pneumonia, especially in its first stage, agglutinating the walls of the cells and bronchioles, which may be brought into contact or close proximity at the end of the act of expiration. The separation of the walls thus agglutinated, in the act of inspiration, gives rise to an auscultatory sign (the crepitant rale) which is diagnostic of vesicular, in distinction from interstitial, pneumonia, known also as lobar and croupous pneumonia.

An accumulation of serum within the air vesicles constitutes the condition called pulmonary œdema. This condition gives rise to signs furnished by percussion and auscultation.

Liquid within the bronchial tubes (serum, pus, blood, or thin mucus) is a condition incident to pulmonary œdema, abscess either of the lung or situated elsewhere and evacuating through the bronchial tubes, phthisis, bronchorrhagia, pneumorrhagia, bronehorrhaœ, and bronchitis. The passage of air through the different varieties of liquid in the tubes, causes bubbling sounds which are appreciable in auscultation. The apparent size of the bubbles (coarseness or fineness) denotes the size of the tubes in which they are produced, and the pitch of the bubbling sounds denotes either solidification or otherwise of the pulmonary substance surrounding the tubes in which the bubbles are produced. Bubbling sounds more intense and on a larger scale are caused by the presence of liquid within the trachea and larynx, known as the tracheal rales or the death rattle.

Diminished calibre of the bronchial tubes within the lungs, either localized or diffused, is a condition due to the presence of tenacious mucus, and the swelling of the mucous membrane in cases of bronchitis. In cases of so-called capillary bronchitis the condition may involve an alarming degree of obstruction. The same condition is incident to bronchial spasm in asthma, occasioning in this disease great suffering, but without immediate danger. The condition is represented by auscultatory signs which enable the auscultator to differentiate the obstruction due to capillary bronchitis from that due to bronchial spasm. Permanent obliteration of more or less of the bronchial tubes is an occasional condition.

Obstruction of a bronchial tube, either within or without the lung, is a condition involving the loss of respiratory sound within the area of the bronchial branches and vesicles not receiving air in consequence of the obstruction. The obstruction may be temporary, being caused by a plug of mueus of sufficient size to prevent the passage of air; the condition is then incident to bronchitis. One of the primary bronchi may be obstructed temporarily by a plug of mucus; and obstruction of the larynx in childhood thus produced may be sufficient to cause death by suffocation.

The inhalation of foreign bodies is another cause of obstruction within the larynx, trachea, or bronchi. A primary bronchus or the trachea may be pressed upon by an aneurismal or other tumor, and, in this way, more or less obstruction to the passage of air is produced. However produced, the situation of the obstruction and its degree are, in general, determinable by means of auscultatory signs.

Dilatation of bronchial tubes occasions two physical conditions differing as regards their auscultatory signs, namely, 1st, an enlargement of greater or less extent, the tubes preserving their cylindrical form; and 2d, a sacculated enlargement. The former occurs generally in connection with solidification around the tubes from hyperplasia of the areolar tissue, and is thus incident to interstitial pneumonia. The latter may give rise to signs which represent pulmonary cavities.

Sacculated dilatations of bronchial tubes, and the cavities incident to phthisis, pulmonary abscess, and circumscribed gangrene of lung, are represented by well-marked and highly distinctive signs furnished by percussion and auscultation. The signs denote either that cavities have flaccid walls which collapse in expiration, and expand in inspiration, or that, owing to solidification of lung, they remain open in both acts of respiration.

More or less of the space within the chest, which, normally, is occupied by lung, may be encroached upon by aneurisms or other intra-thoracic tumors. This is a physical condition giving rise to notably morbid signs furnished by percussion and auscultation.

Finally, an extremely rare morbid physical condition is the presence of more or less of the hollow viscera of the abdomen within the chest, in consequence of a congenital deficiency in the diaphragm, constituting diaphragmatic hernia.

The foregoing morbid physical conditions relate to the respiratory system. Those relating to the heart are deferred, in order that they may precede more immediately an account of the signs of cardiac disease. As a requirement for the study of morbid physical signs, the foregoing morbid physical conditions must be understood arid memorized. To assist the student in the latter, a summary of these conditions is appended.

Summary of Morbid Physical Conditions Incident

to Diseases of the Respiratory System.

1. An accumulation of liquid, serous or purulent, sufficient to fill the affected side of the chest, and sometimes causing more or less enlargement.

2. An accumulation of liquid partially filling the affected side of the chest, the quantity being either small, moderate, or considerable.

3. Exudation of lymph on the pleural surface.

4. Air with liquid within the pleural cavity, and perforation of lung.

5. Air without liquid in the pleural cavity, and perforation.

6. Solidification of lung, either complete or approximating to completeness.

7. Solidification of lung slight or moderate in degree.

8. Dilatation of the air vesicles involving within them an abnormal accumulation of air.

9. Extravasation of air within the pulmonary areolar structure.

10. Viscid exudation within the air vesicles and the bronchioles.

11. Liquid in the air vesicles.

12. Liquid (mucus, serum pus, or blood) within bronchial tubes of large, medium, or small size.

13. Liquid within bronchial tubes of minute size.

14. Obstruction of the pulmonary bronchial tubes by mucus, swelling of the mucous membrane, and spasm of the bronchial muscular fibres.

15. Obstruction of larynx, trachea, or bronchi exterior to the lungs, by plugs of mucus or foreign bodies.

16. Obstruction of the trachea or a primary bronchus by aneurismal or other tumors.

17. Dilatation of bronchial tubes, cylindrical or sacculated.

18. Pulmonary cavities.

19. Tumor within the chest.

20. Diaphragmatic hernia.

The Distinctive Characters of Healthy and Morbid Signs.

For the practice of percussion and auscultation, it is essential to be able to recognize the signs severally which represent the different physical conditions in health and disease. It is essential to distinguish the morbid from the healthy signs, and to discriminate from each other the signs of disease. This recognition and discrimination of signs require a knowledge of the distinctive characters belonging to each of them. In entering upon the study of the signs, therefore, it is a necessary requirement to know whence their distinctive characters are derived. To this point of inquiry the attention of the student is now invited.

The signs being sounds, they are to be recognized and discriminated in the way in which we practically recognize and discriminate other sounds. It is not necessary, in order to do this, to study the science of acoustics. In becoming familiar with other sounds, for example, musical notes produced by different instruments, or the varieties of the human voice, we do not have recourse to that science. It suffices for all practical purposes to contrast the sounds, obtained by percussion and auscultation, with reference to very simple and obvious differences; and, yet, it is necessary to understand very clearly in what these differences consist, or, in other words, the sources of the distinctive characters of these sounds. The more important of the differences between the sounds obtained by percussion and auscultation relate to intensity, pitch, and quality. The distinctive characters of most of the signs are derived from these three sources. In becoming practically acquainted with the signs, they are to be contrasted as regards intensity, pitch, and quality, precisely as we would bring other sounds into contrast in these three aspects. The distinctive characters of the signs, severally, are especially derived from their differences in these respects. The distinctions expressed by the terms intensity, pitch, and quality, are, therefore, to be made clear.

Differences in the intensity of sounds are easily understood. One sound is more intense than another sound when it is simply louder, and varying degrees of intensity are expressed by such terms as feeble or weak and loud, to which may be prefixed adjectives of quality, like very, moderate, etc. This is all that need be said with reference to the first of the three aspects under which sounds are contrasted. It will be seen hereafter that intensity is an essential clement in the distinctive characters of certain of the signs.

Differences in the pitch of sounds are easily understood by those who have given any attention to music. The differences are expressed by the terms high and low, to which may be prefixed words denoting a greater or less degree of highness or lowness. A nice appreciation of variations in the pitch of musical notes, requires what is known as a "musical ear;" but a very nice appreciation is not essential in comparing, as regards pitch, the sounds studied in percussion and auscultation. For the most part, these sounds are not musical notes; nevertheless, differences in pitch are readily perceived. A musical ear is undoubtedly an advantage in readily distinguishing differences in pitch; but by no means a *sine qua non.* For those who have given no attention to music, some difficulty may be at first experienced in judging correctly of differences in this aspect; but the difficulty disappears after a little practice. Differences in pitch now enter pretty largely into the distinctive characters of physical signs; but by Laennec, and those who immediately followed him, comparatively little attention was paid to the study of the signs in this aspect. The writer was led to engage in this study a quarter of a century ago, and hereafter in giving an account of the different signs be will claim to have been the first to have clearly indicated certain characters derived from this source[1].

Differences relating to quality are apt, at first, to be confounded with those relating to pitch; hence the distinction between pitch and quality must be clearly understood. We may say of the quality of a sound, that it embraces whatever is not embraced in the terms intensity and pitch. This is true as a general statement. The sense of the term quality, in distinction from intensity and pitch, may be most readily made clear by an illustration. Let it be supposed that, we hear the notes of an instrument which is unseen—the performer, for example, being in another room. We recognize at once the instrument by the notes, provided it be one with which we are familiar, such as a violin, a flute, a clarionet, etc. We do not need to see the instrument; we recognize it by the sounds. Now, how do we recognize it? Certainly not by the intensity of the sounds; it matters not whether these be loud or weak, so that we hear them. Certainly not by the pitch; for if a piece of music be performed, we get both high and low notes. We recognize the instrument by the quality of the sounds. Each musical instrument, owing to its peculiarity of construc-

---

1 **Vide** Prize Essay on "Variations of Pitch in Percussion and Respiratory Sounds, and their Application to Physical Diagnosis." Transactions of the American Medical Association, 1852.

tion, yields sounds which are peculiar to it; and after we have become familiar with the quality of sound peculiar to any instrument, we immediately thereby recognize it. Precisely in the same way we may recognize certain sounds produced by percussion and auscultation in health and disease. The signs differ in quality according to the physical conditions which they severally represent; and differences in quality will be found hereafter to constitute essential and obvious distinctions by which the signs of health and disease are recognized and discriminated. This is a source of some of the most distinctive of the characters of some of the physical signs.

Of the peculiar quality of any particular sound one can form no definite idea otherwise than by direct observation. That is to say, no one could describe to another the peculiar quality of a particular sound so that it would be clearly apprehended without the sound having been heard. Imagine the attempt to describe the sound of a violin to a person who had never listened to the notes from that instrument—it would be impossible to give a correct idea of it in language. The only way in which an approximative idea could be conveyed in words, would be by comparing the quality to that of some other instrument to the notes of which there was some resemblance—that is, by analogy. To attempt to describe the quality of sounds to one who had never heard them, would be like describing colon to one blind. It will be seen hereafter that the quality of certain sounds obtained by percussion and auscultation is peculiar to them, and their distinctive characters in this aspect can be known only Indirect observation; they cannot be learned by means of any verbal description, nor by any comparisons—that is, by analogy.

Appreciable variations in the quality of sounds are infinite. This may be illustrated by the human voice. Almost every person may be recognized from a peculiar quality of the voice by one who is familiar with it; and the voices of thousands of persons, if compared, would present shades of difference—in fact, as is well known, it is extremely rare for the voices of any two persons to be so nearly identical in quality that they cannot be distinguished from each other. As the diversities in quality of different sounds cannot be described, so they can only be designated by names which are significant from certain resemblances, Terms based on analogies which are used to denote qualities of the sounds furnished by percussion and auscultation are the following: rough, harsh and rude, soft, blowing, hollow, musical, moist, dry, bubbling, gurgling, crackling, clicking, rubbing, grating, creaking, tubular, cracked metal, sibilant or whistling, sonorous or snoring. All these names owe their significance to resemblances to other sounds. One sound furnished both by percussion and auscultation has a qualify which is *sui generis,* and the term used to distinguish it is derived from its source, namely, the vesicular resonance, and the vesicular murmur of respiration.

In addition to intensity, pitch, and quality as sources of the distinctive characters of the signs furnished by percussion and auscultation, there are some other points of difference; namely, the duration of certain sounds, their continuousness or otherwise, their apparent nearness to or distance from the ear, and their strong resemblance to particular sounds, such as the bleating of the goat, the chirping of birds, etc. These points of difference are of lesser importance, the more important by far relating to intensity, pitch, and quality.

The study of the different sounds furnished by percussion and auscultation, with reference to distinctive characters relating especially to intensity, pitch, and quality, distinct signs being determined from points of difference as regards these characters, may be distinguished as the analytical method. It may be so distinguished in contrast with the determination of signs by deductively taking as a standpoint either the physical conditions incident to diseases or the sounds. If we undertake to decide, *a priori,* that certain sounds must be produced by percussion and auscultation when certain conditions are present, we shall be led into error; and so, equally, if we undertake to conclude from the nature of the sounds that they must represent certain conditions. The only reliable method is to analyze the sounds with reference to differences relating especially to intensity, pitch, and quality, and to determine different signs by these differences, the import of each of the signs being then established by the constancy of association with physical conditions. It is by this analytical method only that the distinctive characters of signs can be accurately and clearly ascertained. This is to be borne in mind by the student in physical exploration. He is to become acquainted with the different signs, and to recognize them in practice, by acquiring a knowledge, of the distinctive characters of each, as derived mainly from differences relating to intensity, pitch, and quality. The individuality of the signs, severally, can rest on no other solid basis.

The Significance of the Signs as regards the Physical Conditions which they severally represent.

Knowledge of the significance of the physical signs is the complemental requirement in the study of percussion and auscultation. For the successful employment of these methods, in addition to the recognition of each sign by its distinctive characters, must be known its significance, that is, the physical condition which it represents. In this respect the signs may be compared to the substantives in language, each having a definite signification. The sign furnished by these methods may be said to constitute a language with a very small vocabulary; or taking as the stand-point the things signified, the different physical conditions manifest or express themselves by means of the signs.

It is to be noted that the significance of the morbid signs relates immediately, not to diseases, but to the physical conditions incident thereto. Very few signs are directly diagnostic of any particular disease. They represent conditions not peculiar to one but common to several diseases. Thus, solidification of lung exists in pneumonia, phthisis, pleurisy with effusion, collapse, and pulmonary cancer, and certain signs tell us that this condition exists, together with its situation, its degree, and its extent. With this information the diagnosis of the disease is made by connecting with it pathological laws, together with the history and symptoms. The student in physical exploration should by no means imagine that, for the diagnosis of diseases, exclusive reliance is to be placed on the signs; they are always to be taken in connection with pathological laws, the history, and the symptoms. Disconnected from these, the signs would often lead to error, and it is no disparagement to physical diagnosis that its reliability depends on other facts than those which belong exclusively to it.

To repeat a statement already made more than once, the significance of the signs, as regards the conditions which they severally represent, is based on the constancy of their association with the latter, our knowledge of this association being

Regional Divisions of the Chest.

Before entering on the study of physical exploration, the student should become acquainted with the divisions of the surfaces of the anterior, posterior, and lateral aspects of the chest into circumscribed spaces which are called regions. These divisions, deriving their boundaries and names from their anatomical relations, are sufficiently simple.

Anteriorly the chest is divided into regions as follows: The supra or post-clavicular, the clavicular, the infra-clavicular, the mammary, and the infra-mammary regions. The supra or post-clavicular region extends from the clavicle upward a short distance, corresponding to the variable height to which the lung rises above this bone. The clavicular region embraces the space occupied by the clavicle. The infra-clavicular region embraces the space between the clavicle and the third rib. The mammary region is bounded above by the third and below by the sixth rib, and the infra-mammary region is the portion of the chest below the sixth rib.

Posteriorly the divisions are into the scapular, the infra-scapular, and inter-scapular regions. The scapular region is the space occupied by the scapula, and is divided by the spinous ridge into the upper and lower scapular space. The infra-scapular region is the portion below a horizontal line at the lower angle of the scapula. The inter-scapular region is the space between the posterior margin of the scapula and the spinal column.

Laterally there are two regions, namely, the axillary and the infra-axillary. The axillary region is the space above a horizontal line extending from the lower border of the mammary region, i.e., the sixth rib. The infra-axillary region is the portion below the axillary region.

The portion of the anterior surface occupied b the sternum is divided into the upper and the lower sternal region, the space above the sternal notch being the supra-sternal region.

In order to become familiar with the foregoing regional divisions, it is recommended to the student to delineate them with ink on the chest of the living subject or a cadaver.

It is advisable to study sections, extending from the surface to the centre of the chest, corresponding to the different regions, so as to become familiar with the relation of each section to the parts contained within it. An enumeration of the more important of the anatomical relations of the different regions is as follows:—

1. ***Supra clavicular Region.***—This is relative to the upper extremity or apex of the lung which rises above the clavicle in different persons from half an inch to an inch and a half. The height is generally greater on one side, and this side is usually the left.

2. ***Clavicular Region.***—A small portion of the lung at or near the apex is contained in the section corresponding to this region.

3. ***Infra-clavicular Region.***—The parts situated here are the upper portion of the lung, the lower part of the trachea, with its bifurcation, and the primary bronchi. The bifurcation is on a level with the second rib. The differences between the two primary bronchi, as regards direction, size, and length, are important points in the study of this section.

4. ***Mammary Region.***—The differences between the two sides in the sections corresponding to this region are important. These differences relate especially to the pracordia, and are especially involved in the physical diagnosis of enlargement of the heart. The commencement of the interlobar fissures are in this region. On the left side the fissure is between the fourth and fifth ribs. On the right side the fissure between the upper and middle lobes begins at the fourth costal cartilage, and between the middle and lower lobes a short distance below. The situations of the fissures, however, differ considerably during the acts of inspiration and expiration.

5. ***Infra-mammary Region.***—This region differs in its anatomical relations considerably on the two sides of the chest. On the right side the liver pushes upward the diaphragm nearly or quite to the upper boundary, namely, the sixth rib. On the left side the section corresponding to the region embraces, together with the anterior portion of the lower lob of the lung, portions of the stomach, spleen, and the left lobe of the liver. The variable volume of the stomach at different times occasions considerable variations in the relative spaces occupied by these different parts.

6. ***Supra-sternal Region.***—This region is in relation to the trachea.

7. ***The Upper Sternal Region.***—The bifurcation of the trachea is beneath the

sternum at the centre of a line connecting the second ribs. Below this line the lungs on the two sides are nearly in contact at the mesial line, covering the primary bronchi.

8. *Lower Sternal Region.*—The sternum in this region covers a large portion of the right and a little of the left ventricle.

9. *Scapular Region.*—The section corresponding to this region contains the posterior portion of the upper lobe and a portion of the upper part of the lower lobe of the lung. At the upper part of the lower scapular space, terminates the fissure separating the upper and the lower lobe. The line of this fissure pursues an oblique course to the fourth or fifth rib on the anterior aspect of the chest.

10. *Infra-scapular Region.*—On the right side the lung extends from the upper boundary of this region to the eleventh rib, the liver rising to the latter point. On the left side the section contains a portion of the spleen.

11. *Inter-scapular Region.*—The trachea extends in this section to the fourth dorsal vertebra, where it bifurcates. Below this point, on the two sides, are situated the primary bronchi.

12. *Axillary Region.*—The section corresponding to this region contains a portion of the upper lobo with large bronchial tubes.

13. *Infra-axillary Region.*—This is in relation to the upper part of the liver on the right side, and on the left side to a portion of the spleen and stomach, the remainder of the section occupied by lung.

It is recommended to the student to become familiar with the sections corresponding to the different regions, by dissections for this purpose, and the study of anatomical illustrations.

Asking the student's careful attention to the introductory considerations which have been presented, percussion and auscultation in health and disease, and the physical signs involved in the diagnosis of diseases of the respiratory system and of the heart, will be considered as follows: Chapter II., Percussion in Health; Chapter III., Percussion in Disease; Chapter IV., Auscultation in Health; Chapter V., Auscullation in Disease; Chapter VI., The Physical Diagnosis of the Diseases of the Respiratory System; Chapter VII., The Physical Conditions of the Heart in Health and Disease; Chapter VIII., The Physical Diagnosis of Diseases of the Heart, and, as properly embraced in the scope of this treatise, Chapter IX. will be devoted to the

CHAPTER II.
PERCUSSION IN HEALTH.

Percussion with the fingers or with a percussor and pleximeter—The normal vesicular resonance on percussion; its distinctive characters relating to intensity, pitch, and quality—Variations in the characters of the normal vesicular resonance in different persons—Relations of the pitch of resonance to the vesicular quality—Tympanitic resonance over the abdomen—Variations of the normal resonance in the different regions of the chest—Enumeration of the regions in which the resonance on the two sides varies, and those in which it is identical in health—Influence of age on the normal resonance—Influence of the acts of respiration on the resonance—Rules in the practice of percussion.

PERCUSSION may be performed with either the fingers or artificial instruments. The fingers suffice for the study and in ordinary practice. Instruments are preferable only when it is desired to produce sounds to be heard at some distance, as in class illustrations, and when, from the number of patients to be percussed, as in dispensary or hospital practice, the frequent repetition of the blows renders the fingers tender and painful. The instruments are a pleximeter and a percussor. The simplest and most convenient pleximeter is an oval disk of ivory or hard India-rubber, with projecting handles or auricles, sufficiently large and roughened on their outer aspect, so as to be conveniently held by the fingers. The best percussor is a double cone of caoutchouc inclosed by a metallic ring, to which is attached a rod of metal with a wooden handle of convenient length, weight, and size. This instrument is very durable. When percussion is performed with the fingers, the palmar surface of one or more of those of the left hand should be applied to the chest, with pressure sufficient to condense the soft structures, and the blows are given with one or more of the fingers of the right hand bent at the second phalangeal joint so as to form a right angle. In giving the blows, the movements should be limited to the wrist-joint, the ends, not the pulp, of the percussing fingers being brought into contact with the dorsal surface of the finger, or fingers, applied to the chest. The percussing fingers should be withdrawn instantly the blow is given. The type of perfect percussion is the movement of the hammers when the keys of a piano-forte are struck. The force of the percussion should never be sufficient to give pain to the patient; generally either light, or moderately forcible blows suffice. The requisite tact in the performance of percussion is acquired by a little practice.

The first object in the study of percussion is to become acquainted with the characters which are distinctive of the sound obtained thereby from the healthy chest. For this object, the percussion be made either in front in the infra-clavicular region of either side, or behind in the infra-scapular region, the sound in these situations being louder than in other regions. Percussion being performed, a sound or a resonance is produced. This sound or resonance is now to be analyzed with reference to characters derived from intensity, pitch, and quality. What are these characters? The intensity will depend, other things being equal, on the force of the blow; the resonance is comparatively feeble with a slight, and loud with a strong percussion. Other circumstances affect the intensity, irrespective of the force of the blow, namely, the volume of the lung, the elasticity of the costal cartilages, and the thickness of the soft part which cover the chest. Owing to these circumstances, the intensity of the resonance is by no means similar, in the same situation, in all healthy persons; it is comparatively feeble in some and loud in others. There is nothing distinctive of this normal resonance to be derived from intensity, and we say, therefore, that the intensity is variable.

What is the pitch of this normal resonance? The pitch of a sound is always relative; and, comparing this resonance with all the morbid signs obtained by percussion, it is lower in pitch. We say, therefore, that the pitch of this normal resonance is low. The pitch, however, is found to vary in different healthy persons.

What is the quality of this normal resonance? It has a quality which is peculiar to it. In this respect it is not identical with any sound produced otherwise than by percussion over healthy lung either within or without the chest. The qualify cannot, therefore, be learned by analogy, nor can it be described; it can only be appreciated by direct observation. The peculiar quality is due to the fact that the resonance is from air contained in the pulmonary vesicles. This arrangement causes the peculiar quality, just as the construction of any particular musical instrument causes the quality or tone peculiar to that instrument; hence, as it is convenient to give the quality a name, we call it the ***vesicular quality.*** This quality is not equally marked in all healthy persons, being, as a rule, more marked in proportion to the intensity of the resonance.

The normal resonance, then, obtained by percussion, may be thus defined:—

A resonance of variable intensity, low in pitch and having a peculiar quality called vesicular. The word vesicular is frequently embraced in the name of this healthy sign; we call it the normal resonance, the normal pulmonary resonance, or the normal vesicular resonance. The last of these names is to be preferred.

The normal vesicular resonance on percussion, as has been seen, is not uniform in all healthy persons; not only is its intensity variable, but it varies in pitch and in the amount of vesicular quality. This may be easily illustrated, by percussing successively in the same situation, and with the same force, a series of persons who are assumed to be free from disease. Is there not in this fact an obstacle in practically determining this healthy sign? The fact occasions no embarrassment for this reason: we determine, in each case, that the resonance is normal by a comparison of the two sides of the chest, per-cussing in corresponding situations on the two sides and with the same force. There is no abstract standard of the normal vesicular resonance, but, by comparing the two sides of the chest, the standard of health proper to each person is obtained. The laws of disease are such that, for all practical purposes, the standard of health is in this way almost always available. Notwithstanding the variations within the range of health, the lowness in pitch and the vesicular quality are sufficiently distinctive of this normal sign as compared with the morbid signs.

The pitch of the vesicular resonance and its vesicular quality are in a uniform relation to each other; that is, the conditions giving rise to the peculiar quality, also render the pitch low. In proportion as the vesicular quality is marked, the pitch is lowered, and, conversely, with diminution of the vesicular quality the pitch is relatively higher. This relation between the pitch and quality will be found to hold good in the resonance modified by disease as well as in health. Another relation may be here stated, namely, whenever, in health or disease, a tympanitic quality is combined with the vesicular, and in proportion as the former predominates, the pitch of the resonance is raised.

The pitch and quality of the normal vesicular resonance may be readily illustrated by percussing successively over the chest and the abdomen. The different sections of the alimentary canal, generally containing more or less gas, a resonance is obtained by percussion over the abdomen. This resonance is, of course, devoid of the vesicular quality; in contradistinction to the latter its quality is called tympanitic. This tympanitic resonance is not uniform in all parts of the abdomen, but everywhere the quality is tympanitic, that is, non-vesicular, and the pitch is everywhere higher than that of the normal vesicular resonance. The tympanitic resonance over the stomach is generally high in pitch, and frequently has a ringing or metallic intonation. The gastric tympanitic resonance, recognized by these characters, will be found to be involved frequently in sounds produced by percussing over the chest. Gas in the cæcum gives a still higher pitch of resonance. Over the colon the resonance is lower than over the cæcum and stomach, and it is still lower over the small intestines. In all these situations, bringing the tympanitic in contrast with the normal vesicular resonance, the peculiar quality of the latter and its lowness of pitch are rendered apparent. The term tympanitic resonance will be found to enter into the names of two of the morbid signs obtained by percussion.

Having studied the characters of the normal vesicular resonance, and become practically familiar with them by percussing different healthy persons, the student should study the variations which this resonance presents in the different regions of the chest. In doing this he acquires more and more tact in the performance of percussion, and becomes more and more familiar with the characters in general of the normal vesicular resonance.

Supra- or Post-clavicular Region.—The resonance here varies much in intensity in different persons. The vesicular quality is most marked in the central portions. Toward the sternal extremity the resonance acquires a tympanitic quality from the proximity to the trachea; it becomes vesiculo-tympanitic, a term which will be applied to one of the morbid signs.

Clavicular Region.—Near the sternum the resonance is somewhat tympanitic from the proximity to the trachea. At the central portion the vesicular quality is more or less marked, and the intensity is diminished at the acromial extremity.

Infra-clavicular Region.—The resonance in this region is more intense than elsewhere, excepting the axillary and the infra-scapular regions. The vesicular quality is combined with a tympanitic quality toward the sternum, the latter being derived from the primary and secondary bronchi. As always when the vesicular and the tympanitic quality are combined, the pitch is raised. This combination in health and disease is recognized by the intensity, pitch, and quality.

Scapular Region.—The resonance in this region is notably less intense than in the infra-clavicular region, owing to the presence of the scapula and its muscles. In proportion as the intensity is less, the vesicular quality is less marked. The resonance in health, however, is quite sufficient for morbid signs to be available in this situation.

Inter-scapular Region.—The resonance in this region is weak in comparison with other regions, owing to the muscles which here cover the chest. In the upper part of the region the resonance is somewhat tympanitic from the relation to the trachea and bronchi.

Mammary Region.—The right and the left mammary region are to be studied with reference to differences relating to the liver and the heart. On the right side, from the fourth rib downward, the resonance is diminished, the convex extremity of the liver extending up to this height. At or a little below the lower border of this region on the mammary line, that is, a vertical line passing through the nipple, resonance ceases, the lower lobe of the right lung not extending below this point. Between the third and fifth ribs on this side near the sternum the resonance is diminished from the presence of a portion of the right auricle and ventricle. On the left side the resonance is diminished within the præcordial space. This space extends vertically from the third rib to the fifth intercostal space, and horizontally from the sternum to a point at or a little within the mammary line. The resonance is considerably diminished within what is called the superficial cardiac space. This space is represented by a right-angled triangle, the right angle formed by a vertical line drawn from a point on the median line intersected by a horizontal line connecting the fourth ribs, and a horizontal line intersecting the point of apex beat in the fifth intercostal space; an oblique line drawn from the centre of the sternum on a level with the fourth rib and the point of apex beat forms the hypothenuse of the right-angled triangle. Within this space the heart is in contact with the thoracic wall. Without this space and within the præcordia the heart is covered with lung, and the resonance on percussion is less diminished. It is a useful exercise for the student, to observe the diminution of the area of the superficial cardiac space by a forced inspiration, and the increase of this area by a forced expiration, as determined by percussion. Aside from the presence of the heart and the convex extremity of the liver, the resonance over the mammary is less than in the infra-clavicular region, being diminished by the pectoral muscle which varies considerably in bulk in different persons, and in women by the mammary gland, the size of the latter varying very much in different women. The development of the mammas, however, is never so great as to preclude the useful employment of percussion in this region.

Infra-mammary Region.—In this region, as in the region above it, the two sides present notable differences owing to the situation of organs below the diaphragm. On the right side, over the greater part, and sometimes the whole of this region, resonance is wanting, that is, percussion gives flatness. It is easy to delineate the boundary between the lower border of the right lung and the liver, or, as it is called, **the line of hepatic flatness.** It is also easy to distinguish over this line the height to which the lower extremity of the liver extends, or, as it is called, **the line of hepatic dulness.** The situation of both these lines varies considerably in different healthy persons. The distance between the two lines is from one to ten inches. Both lines are affected considerably by a forced inspiration and a forced expiration. A forced inspiration depresses the line o flatness about one and a half inches. A forced expiration causes the line to rise from two and a half to five and a half inches. The distance, therefore, between this line at the end of a forced expiration, and at the end of a forced inspiration varies from four to seven inches. With reference to the practice of percussion, as well as for the purpose of verification, these points should be studied. Not infrequently percussion over the right infra-mammary region yields a tympanitic resonance due to the distension with gas to the transverse colon.

On the left side, the resonance in this region varies in different persons, in the same person at different times, and in different portions of the region at the same time, the variations depending on the organs below the diaphragm. Flatness is caused by the extension of the left lobe of the liver into this region about ten inches to the left of the median line. The left portion of the region is in relation to the spleen, an organ which varies considerably in size in health as well as disease, its average dimensions being about four inches in length and three inches in width. Between the spleen and the liver lies the stomach, the volume of which is constantly fluctuating, owing to its varying solid, liquid, and gaseous contents. Distension of the stomach with gas occasions a tympanitic resonance which frequently is transmitted above into the mammary region in health as well as in disease. The space corresponding to the spleen is determined by the vesicular resonance above and the tympanitic resonance below, the latter boundary, however, not being very reliable on account of the ready conduction of tympanitic resonance for a certain distance. The distension of the stomach with solid or liquid contents of course occasions flatness. The study of the infra-mammary regions with reference to the variations in resonance arising from the relations to the organs below the diaphragm, is of much utility from the practice, as well as the knowledge, which it involves. The exercise of endeavoring to define the boundaries of these different organs in healthy persons, will be of great service to the student in acquiring tact in percussion, and in discriminating differences in the sounds obtained by this method.

Sternal Regions.—In the upper sternal region, that is, above the lower margin of the second rib, the resonance is non-vesicular, being derived from air in the trachea above the point of bifurcation. Being non-vesicular, it is, of course, tympanitic, this term embracing all sounds which are devoid of the vesicular quality. Between the second and third ribs, the inner borders of the two lungs approximating, the resonance has a vesicular quality more or less marked; but owing to the remnant of the thymus gland, together with adipose substance, and the presence of the large vessels, the resonance is not intense in this situation. Below the third rib the resonance has modifications due to the combination of several different organs situated beneath the lower sternal region. On the right side of the mesial line is the inner border of the right lung, the greater part of the right and a portion of the left ventricle of the heart lying beneath; a portion of the liver extends into the lower part of this region, and a portion of the stomach when distended. The resonance thus varies in different situations, and often presents a mixed character. It is a useful exercise to endeavor to define by percussion the boundaries of the several organs which are here in juxtaposition.

Infra-scapular Regions.—The resonance below the scapula is intense as compared with that over the scapula, and the vesicular quality is marked. The resonance extends to the eleventh rib which is the lower boundary of the lung. On the right side, at or near this point, is the line of hepatic flatness, hepatic dulness extending from one to two inches above this line. The line of hepatic flatness and of hepatic dulness is lowered from one to two inches by a deep inspiration, and raised by a forced expiration. On the left side the resonance may receive a tympanitic quality from the presence of gas in the stomach.

Lateral Regions.—In these regions the resonance is relatively intense, and notably vesicular. On the right side the line of hepatic flatness is at the eighth rib, hepatic dulness extending above this line as in front and behind. On the left side the resonance may be rendered somewhat, dull by the presence of the spleen, but it oftener acquires a tympanitic quality from the presence of gas in the stomach.

As has been stated, the normal vesicular resonance is not in all persons identical as regards intensity, pitch, and quality. There is, therefore, no fixed standard in these respects by which we can determine whether the resonance be normal or not. The standard proper to each person is to be ascertained by a comparison of the two sides of the chest; each person, in other words, furnishes his own standard of health. But, it is to be observed, that all the regions do not normally correspond in respect of the resonance on the two sides. In the following regions the resonance is notably dissimilar on the two sides: The mammary, the infra-mammary, the infra-axillary, and the infra-scapular. On the other hand, in the following regions the resonance on the two sides is nearly or quite identical: The supra-clavicular, clavicular and infra-clavicular, the scapular and inter-scapular, and the axillary. In some of the latter the resonance has normally some points of disparity, and it is of practical importance to note the small dissimilarity which thus belongs to health. This statement applies especially to the infra-clavicular region, a region which, as will be seen hereafter, is of great importance with reference to the signs of phthisis. In this region the resonance on the left side is somewhat more intense, more vesicular, and lower in pitch than the resonance on the right side; ***per contra,*** the resonance is less intense, less vesicular, and higher on the right side. This disparity is observable in all persons, but is more marked in some than in others. The student should become practically familiar with this normal difference between the two sides, and in becoming so, the practical experience acquired in performing percussion will be of use.

The normal resonance is affected by age. In early life, when the costal cartilages are flexible and elastic, the resonance is more intense and lower in pitch than in old age when the cartilages are rigid, and the vesicular structure of the lung more or less atrophied.

The resonance varies considerably in the different regions at the end of a full inspiration and at the end of a forced expiration. With regard to this disparity, the following is an extract from a work on physical exploration, published by the author in 1856:—

"The percussion-sound may also be found to vary at different periods of an act of respiration in the same individual. The quantity of air contained within the air-cells, and consequently the relative proportion of air and solids, are by no means equal after a full inspiration and after a forced expiration. This difference in lung expansion may occasion an appreciable disparity in resonance, according as the percussion is made at the conclusion of a full inspiration, or a forced expiration. The disparity is not appreciable uniformly in different persons. This fact I have ascertained by noting the results of examinations made with reference to the point. When it does exist, it usually consists, contrary to what might perhaps have been anticipated, and the reverse of what is usually stated in works on physical exploration, in diminished resonance and elevation of pitch at the conclusion of inspiration. This is probably to be explained by the greater degree of tension of the lungs and thoracic walls produced by inspiration voluntarily prolonged and maintained—a condition presenting physical obstacles to sonorous vibrations more than sufficient to counterbalance the increased proportion of air within the cells. It is a curious fact, worthy of notice, that the two sides of the chest are not always found to be affected equally as regards the percussion-sound, at the conclusion of a full inspiration, contrasted with that after a forced expiration. I have observed the contrast to be more striking on the right than on the left side; and in one instance on the left side, the resonance was less intense and somewhat tympanitic after a full inspiration, while on the right side, the opposite effect was produced, and the sound became quite dull after a forced expiration. In view of these variations in a certain proportion of instances incident to different periods of a single act of respiration, in some cases of disease in which it is desirable to observe great delicacy in the correspondence of the two sides, pains should be taken to percuss corresponding points at a similar stage of respiration, and the close of a full inspiration is, perhaps, the period to be preferred. Ordinarily, the liability to error from this source is obviated, either by repeating a series of strokes, first on one side and next on the other, or by percussing both sides repeatedly in quick succession, in order mentally to obtain the average intensity and other characters of the sound during the successive stages of a respiration. The instances of disease, however, are exceedingly rare, in which such nicety of discrimination is important."

Prof. Da Costa has recently studied more fully the variations in this respect in the different regions in disease as well as in health, and he has distinguished this as "respiratory percussion."[2]

Rules in the Practice of Percussion.

1. Prior to a comparison of the two sides of the chest, as regards the resonance on percussion, either in health or disease, an examination by inspection should be made, in order to determine whether there be any deviation from the normal conformation. In what has been stated concerning percussion in health, it is assumed that the chest is symmetrical. Want of symmetry may be due to congenital deformities, and to those caused by rachitis, chronic pleurisy, curvature of the spine, and injuries. Any deviation from the normal conformation will affect more or less the resonance in corresponding regions on the two sides. Due allowance is to be made for want of symmetry in determining morbid signs, and often the existence of these cannot be determined with positiveness when there is considerable deformity. The signs obtained by auscultation are less affected by want of symmetry than those obtained by percussion.

2. Attention to the position of the person examined is important with reference to the normal symmetry of the chest. If the person be standing or sitting, the position should be upright and the shoulders brought to a level. A little inclination of the body to one side, or a depression of one shoulder, will be found to affect perceptibly the normal resonance, when the two sides are compared. If the body be recumbent, it should be as near as possible on a level plane. These conditions are

---

2 Vide work on Diagnosis, fourth edition, 1876.

indispensable for a nice comparison of the two sides either in health or disease.

3. In making a nice comparison, the person who percusses should be as nearly as possible directly either in front or behind the person percussed. Percussion made by one standing or sitting by the side of the person percussed, is almost certain to produce an abnormal disparity.

4. Percussion made successively on one side, and the other side, must be in all respects the same, in regard to the mode, the force of the blow, and the situation. A light percussion on one side, and a strong percussion on the other side, will, of course, cause ft disparity in the intensity of resonance. The percussion must be made in succession at points as nearly as possible equidistant from the median line, and from the summit or base of the chest. With reference to great nicety, the percussion, if made on the rib or intercostal space on one aide, must be made on the rib or intercostal space on the other side. Great nicety of comparison also requires that, if the percussion be made on one side during the act of inspiration, it should be made on the other side during this act. The signs of disease, however, are generally so well marked, that very close attention to these points is not necessary.

5. A series of blows in rapid succession (5 or 7) is to be preferred to one or two, in practising percussion, difference in intensity, pitch, and quality being thereby better appreciated.

6. Percussion may be made lightly or forcibly, the former being called superficial, and the latter deep percussion. With light blows the resonance comes from the superficies of the lung, and from within a limited area. With forcible blows the resonance is from a greater depth, and a wider space. The results of these different modes of practising percussion may be illustrated within the præcordia in health. Comparing the resonance over the superficial cardiac space with that in a corresponding situation on the right side, dullness is more marked with light than with forcible blows, the resonance from the latter coming from a wider area. On the other hand, comparing the resonance over the deep cardiac space, dulness is more marked with forcible than with light blows, owing to the presence of lung between the heart and the walls of the chest; this rule is of importance in its application to percussion in disease.

7. Percussion over the anterior portion of the chest, the person percussed leaning against a door, a board partition, or a lathed wall, gives an increased intensity of

_____

CHAPTER III.
PERCUSSION IN DISEASE.

Enumeration of the signs of disease furnished by percussion—Requirements for a practical knowledge of these signs—The distinctive characters of, the morbid physical conditions represented by, and the different diseases into the diagnosis of which enter, these signs, severally, to wit, 1. Absence of resonance or flatness; 2. Diminished resonance or dulness; 3. Tympanitic resonance; 4. Vesiculo-tympanitic resonance; 5. Amphoric resonance; 6. Cracked metal resonance—Sense of resistance felt in the practice of percussion as a morbid sign.

PERCUSSION in disease furnishes signs which represent certain of the morbid physical conditions incident to the different pulmonary affections; with these physical conditions and their relations to pulmonary affections the student is supposed to be familiar (***vide*** page 20 ***et seq.***).

The signs of disease furnished by percussion are resolvable into six, namely: 1. Absence of resonance or flatness; 2. Diminished resonance or dulness; 3. Tympanitic resonance; 4. Vesiculo tympanitic resonance; 5. Amphoric resonance; and 6. Cracked-metal resonance. The two last named signs are properly varieties of tympanitic resonance, but it is most convenient to consider them as distinct signs.

Knowledge of these six signs sufficient for their availability in physical diagnosis requires, ***first***, practical acquaintance with the characters which distinguish each from the others, as well as from the normal resonance; and ***second***, the significance of each, that is, the morbid physical conditions which they severally represent. Under these two aspects the signs will now be considered.

1. Absence of Resonance or Flatness.

This sign is sufficiently denned by its name. It is absence of resonance or sound. Nothing is heard but a noise such as may be produced by percussing over a solid mass, for example a limb composed of muscle and bone, or over a collection of liquid, for example the abdomen in hydro-peritoneum or ascites. There being no resonance or sound, the sign has no characters pertaining to pitch or quality. It may be illustrated on the healthy chest by percussing in the right infra-mammary region below the line of hepatic flatness.

There are four classes of morbid physical conditions giving rise to flatness on percussion, namely, 1st, a certain quantity of liquid in the pleural sac, in the substance of the lungs, or in pulmonary cavities; 2d, liquid filling the air vesicles; 3d, complete solidification of lung; and 4th, a tumor within the chest. Flatness on percussion always represents one of these morbid physical conditions.

These conditions are incident to different diseases, as follows:—

1st. Liquid in the pleural cavity is incident to pleurisy with effusion, empyema, and hydrothorax. A collection of liquefied exudation within the lungs is incident to phthisis. A collection of pus constitutes pulmonary abscess, and phthisical cavities, or those caused by circumscribed gangrene, may become filled with morbid liquid products.

2d. Serous effusion into the air vesicles constitute pulmonary œdema. Liquid blood extravasated characterizes hemorrhagic infarctus, pneumorrhagia or pulmonary apoplexy. Pus infiltrating more or less of the parenchyma may be derived from an abscess either within the lung, or elsewhere, for example the liver, and from the pleural cavity in empyema, when perforation of lung takes place.

3d. Solidification of lung occurs in pneumonia from an exudation within the air cells; it is produced by condensation from compression by liquid or air in the pleural sac, the pressure of a tumor, and by collapse; it exists in cases of phthisis, in interstitial pneumonia, and in carcinomatous infiltration of lung.

4th. Tumors within the chest are of different kinds, for examples, aneurisms and cancerous growths. In proportion to their size they occupy space belonging to the lung, as well as condensing the latter by pressure. Flatness may also be caused by the encroachment of organs situated below the diaphragm upon the thoracic space, as in cases of enlargement of the liver and spleen.

Flatness on percussion in all these conditions is the same. The sign alone does not enable us to discriminate the conditions from each other, or to determine the existing disease.

Finding this sign present, the particular condition and the disease in each case are to be determined by the situation of the flatness, its extent, the associated physical signs furnished by auscultation, together with the other methods of exploration, and by the symptomatic events.

2. Diminished Resonance or Dulness.

The resonance on percussion is diminished, or there is dulness, when the solids or liquids within the chest are morbidly increased without increase in the quantity of air, the increased amount of solids or liquids not being sufficient to cause flatness. Diminution of air, without increase of either solids or liquids, as in collapse of pulmonary lobules, also gives rise to dulness. We may formularize the physical conditions by saying that they consist in an abnormal proportion of solids or liquids over the air in the pulmonary vesicles.

Dulness varies in degree. It may be slight, very slight, moderate, considerable, or great. These adjectives of quantity express sufficiently the variations in this regard. The degree of dulness corresponds to the amount of the relative disproportion of solids or liquids over the air within the chest.

The pitch of sound is higher than that of the normal resonance of the persons percussed. This is invariable; with dulness there is always more or less elevation of pitch. The quality is altered only in amount; there is, of course, less vesicular quality in proportion as the intensity of the resonance is diminished.

The characters which distinguish this sign, thus, are, lessened intensity of resonance, elevation of pitch, and weakened vesicular quality.

The morbid conditions giving rise to this sign are those which, existing in a greater degree, give rise to flatness. Morbid products within the pleural sac, serum, pus, lymph, if not sufficient to cause flatness, give rise to dulness. The sign, therefore, occurs in pleurisy, empyema, and hydrothorax. The same is true of pulmonary œdema, hemorrhagic infarctus, pneumorrhagic and purulent infiltration of lung. Solidification of lung, when not complete, occasions dulness; hence, it is a sign in pneumonia, vesicular and interstitial, in phthisis, in condensation of lung from compression, in collapse of pulmonary lobules, and in carcinomatous infiltration. A tumor within the chest, not sufficiently large to cause flatness, gives rise to dulness.

There are, however, some conditions giving rise to dulness, which are never sufficient to cause flatness. Pulmonary congestion limited to a lobe may diminish the resonance appreciably. Thus dulness may exist in the first stage of pneumonia, before solidification from pneumonic exudation has taken place. A thin layer of lymph upon the pleural surfaces causes dulness after the liquid effusion in pleurisy has been removed, and after the vesicular exudation in pneumonia is absorbed. Dulness may also be caused by a considerable accumulation of mucus or coagulated blood within the intra-pulmonary bronchial tubes.

The particular morbid condition which gives rise to dulness cannot be inferred from the characters of the sign; the sign only denotes that some one of the different conditions exists. The condition which exists in each case, and the disease, are to be determined by the situation, extent, and degree of dulness, taken in connection with the information derived from other methods of exploration than percussion, together with the history and symptoms.

3. Tympanitic Resonance.

Resonance is tympanitic whenever it is entirely devoid of the vesicular quality; in other words, any resonance which is non-vesicular is tympanitic. The leading distinctive character of the preceding sign (dulness) relates to intensity, whereas, the leading distinctive character of this sign relates to quality. Tympanitic resonance derives no distinctive character from intensity; it may be either more or less intense than the resonance of health in the person percussed. This point is to be impressed, inasmuch as with many the idea of a tympanitic resonance involves increased intensity of sound; a resonance, be it never so feeble, if it be non-vesicular, is tympanitic. If, however, the resonance be quite feeble, it is not always easy to determine whether there ho or he not any appreciable vesicular quality. The term used by Stokes, namely, "tympanitic dulness," is properly enough applied to a resonance with diminished intensity, in which a vesicular quality cannot be appreciated. As regards pitch, a tympanitic resonance is higher than the normal vesicular resonance. If there be any exceptions to this rule, they are extremely infrequent. The tympanitic resonance over different parts of the abdomen is always higher in pitch than the resonance over healthy lung.

The following are the morbid physical conditions which give rise to tympanitic resonance:—

1st. Air in the pleural cavity. It is, therefore, a sign of pneumothorax. Frequently, in this affection, the tympanitic resonance is more intense than the resonance of health, the pitch being more or less raised.

2d. Pulmonary cavities containing air. It occurs therefore in cases of phthisis. In this disease the tympanitic resonance is limited to a circumscribed space corresponding to the site and size of the cavity, whereas, in pneumothorax, it frequently exists over a considerable part or the whole of the affected side of the chest.

3d. Complete solidification of the whole or a part of the upper lobe of a lung. The tympanitic resonance, under these circumstances, must be derived from the air in the lower part of the trachea and the bronchial tubes exterior to the lungs. This is the explanation of the sign in the second stage of pneumonia affecting an upper lobe, and in certain cases of phthisis prior to the stage of excavation. Dilatation of the intra-pulmonary bronchial tubes, with solidification surrounding them, as in some cases of interstitial pneumonia or cirrhosis of lung, may give rise to tympanitic resonance.

4th. Conduction of resonance from the stomach or colon containing air or gas. A gastric tympanitic resonance is frequently conducted over a part, and sometimes over the whole of the left side of the chest. This is more likely to occur when the left lung is solidified and rendered thereby a better conductor of sound. On the right side less frequently a tympanitic resonance may be conducted upward from the colon to a greater or less extent.

4. Vesiculo-Tympanitic Resonance.

This name was proposed by the author many years ago to denote a sign with the following distinctive characters: The resonance increased in intensity; the quality, a combination of the vesicular with the tympanitic, and the pitch high in proportion as the tympanitic quality predominates over the vesicular.

This sign represents especially one morbid physical condition, namely, an abnormal accumulation of air in consequence of dilatation of the air vesicles, that is, pulmonary or vesicular emphysema. The sign also is present in interstitial or interlobular emphysema. The relation of the sign to these affections renders it of great value in physical diagnosis.

A vesiculo-tympanitic resonance is obtained, when the pleural sac is partially filled with liquid, by percussing over the lung on the affected side. Although the pressure of the liquid diminishes the volume of the lung, as a rule it yields this sign. The resonance is vesiculo tympanitic above the liquid when the latter is sufficient to fill a third, a half, or even two-thirds of the intra-thoracic space. The sign is also obtained over the upper lobe when the lower lobe is solidified in the second stage of pneumonia, and over the lower lobe when the upper lobe is solidified.

5. Amphoric Resonance.

Resonance is said to be amphoric when it has a musical intonation analogous to that produced by blowing over the mouth of an empty bottle. An amphoric sound is easily illustrated by filliping the cheek made tense, the mouth not completely closed and the jaws separated, as is done when the sound of a liquid flowing from a bottle is imitated. By varying the size of the cavity of the mouth, the amphoric sound thus produced may be made to vary much in pitch. This illustration exemplifies the mechanism of the sign in disease.

The sign represents a pulmonary cavity which is generally phthisical. The conditions, aside from the existence of the cavity, are, rigidity of its walls, so that they do not collapse, the presence, of course, of air within the cavity, and free communication with the bronchial tubes. These accessory conditions are not constant, so that an amphoric resonance over a cavity is sometimes found, and at other times wanting. Directly alter having been wanting, it may be reproduced if the patient expectorate freely.

When percussion, is made with reference to this sign, the mouth of the patient should be open, and one or two rather forcible blows are better than a series of four or six. The amphoric sound may be often distinctly perceived if the ear be brought into close proximity to the patient's open mouth, when the sign is not appreciable otherwise. It may be rendered still more distinct by means of the binaural stethoscope, the pectoral extremity being close to the mouth of the patient.

As a cavernous sign the amphoric resonance is very reliable; but it does not invariably denote pulmonary cavity. It is obtained in some cases of pneumothorax, the pleural space filled with air having a cavity which communicates with the bronchial tubes through a perforation of the lung situated above the level of the liquid. It is some times obtained over a solidified portion of lung situated in close proximity to a primary bronchus, the resonance being derived from the air within the latter.

yielding of the costal cartilages, it may even be produced in health over a primary bronchus. In all these exceptional instances, the associated signs and symptoms will prevent the error of attributing the sign to a pulmonary cavity.

This sign is properly a variety of tympanitic resonance.

6. Cracked-metal Resonance.

The name of this sign, expressing an analogy to the sound produced by striking a cracked metallic vessel, denotes its peculiar character. It may be imitated by folding the hands so as to form a cavity and striking them upon the knee, in the familiar trick of producing in this way a sound as if metal coins were between the palms. This illustration, also, exemplifies the mechanism of the sign. Like the sign last described, the sign is a variety of tympanitic resonance.

The cracked-metal, like the amphoric, resonance represents generally a phthisical cavity. Percussion is to be made in the same way as lor the production of the amphoric resonance, and, like the latter, the Cracked-metal character is often perceived if the ear be brought close to the patient's mouth when otherwise it is not appreciable.

The cracked-metal and the amphoric resonance are often associated; and the statements made with respect to the exceptional instances in which the latter is produced, without the existence of a pulmonary cavity, will apply equally to the former.

In addition to the acoustic phenomena produced by percussion, with the fingers applied to the chest instead of a pleximeter, the percussor can appreciate an abnormal ***sense of resistance*** in certain conditions of disease. In health, with a somewhat forcible percussion, the walls of the chest are felt to yield in proportion as the costal cartilages are flexible. This yielding is diminished or ceases when a collection of liquid in the pleural cavity, or liquid in the air vesicles, and solidification of lung, offer a mechanical obstacle thereto. An abnormal sense of resistance on percussion, thus determinable by comparison of the two sides of the chest, is a sign representing some one of the morbid physical conditions just named. This properly belongs among the signs obtained by palpation. The sign is to be taken in connection with other signs in determining the condition which exists in particular cases.

CHAPTER IV.
AUSCULTATION IN HEALTH.

Importance of the study of the auscultatory sounds in health—Immediate and mediate auscultation—Advantages of the binaural stethoscope—Rules to be observed in auscultation—Divisions of the study of auscultation in health—The normal laryngeal and tracheal respiration—The normal vesicular murmur; its distinctive character; and the variations in the different regions on the same side, and in corresponding regions on the two sides of the chest—The normal vocal resonance—The laryngeal and tracheal voice and whisper—The normal thoracic vocal resonance and fremitus; the distinctive characters of each; the variations in different regions on the same side, and in corresponding regions on the two sides of the chest—The normal bronchial whisper, with its variations in different regions on the same side, and in corresponding regions on the two sides of the chest.

THE term auscultation, limited in its application to the respiratory system, denotes the act of listening to the normal and abnormal sounds produced by respiration, voice, and cough. In this and the next chapter, the method of exploration thus named will be considered in its application to the respiratory system; it will be considered subsequently, as applied to sounds relating to the circulatory system.

The study of auscultatory sounds in health is essential its as preparatory for the study of auscultation in disease. The student must be familiar with the normal sounds before undertaking to become acquainted with those which represent morbid conditions. Ample time and attention should be given to the study of auscultation in health. The omission to do this is a frequent cause of difficulty and want of success in attaining to a satisfactory proficiency in physical diagnosis. The practical tact and skill required in diagnosis may be obtained in advance by devoting sufficient study to the healthy chest before entering on the study of the auscultatory signs of disease. Moreover, as will be seen, some of the most important morbid signs have their-analogues in certain normal sounds pertaining to the respiratory system.

Auscultation is either immediate or mediate. It is immediate when the ear is applied directly to the chest, which may be either denuded or covered with a cloth or more or less of the clothing. It is mediate when the sounds are conducted to the ear by means of an instrument called a stethoscope. The student should practise both immediate and mediate auscultation. The direct application of the ear to the chest suffices for diagnosis in many cases of disease; but there are sometimes objections to this by the patient on the score of delicacy, and by the auscultator on the score of the uncleanliness of the person examined. There are certain parts of the chest which can only be explored by a stethoscope, and this instrument has the advantage of circumscribing the space whence the auscultatory sounds are derived. Moreover, by means of the stethoscope which is to be preferred over the great variety of instruments heretofore in use, the sounds are heard much better than by immediate auscultation.

The stethoscope which is to be preferred conducts the sounds into both ears, that is, it is binaural. In this consists its great superiority. At the present time what is known as Cammann's stethoscope[3] seems to combine more recommendations than any other form of a binaural instrument. The conduction into both ears renders the sounds much louder and more distinct than when they are heard with one ear in cither mediate or immediate auscultation. Another advantage is, the mind is not distracted by sounds entering the ear not employed in auscultation. The advantages, however, of Cammann's stethoscope are not appreciated until after some practice. At first, a bumming sound is heard which divides the attention and thus obscures the intra-thoracic sounds. After a little practice this humming sound is not heeded, and it ceases to be any obstacle. Many who use the instrument only a few times are dissatisfied with it, and discontinue its use, when if they had used it longer they would not have been willing to dispense with it. The author's experience with a

---

3   Invented by the late Dr. Cammann, of New York.

large number of classes in private instruction has been this: at first, most members of a class prefer the ear applied directly to the chest; but, before the course of instruction is ended, the binaural stethoscope is so much preferred that it is difficult to enforce a fair proportion of practice in immediate auscultation.

Another reason for the fact that this stethoscope is not sufficiently appreciated in this country is, many of the instruments sold are defectively made. Unless proper attention has been paid to all the nice points of the stethoscope as devised by Cammann, an instrument is worthless. An instrument must be very good, or it is without any value. The knobs which are to enter the ears must be of the right size; if they enter too far they occasion pain. The curves at the aural extremity must be such that the aperture is in the direction of the meatus of the ear. The flexible tubes must not be stiff, and their movements must be noiseless. All the tubes must be unobstructed, for it is the air within the tubes which chiefly conducts the sounds. In the use of the instrument it should be applied to the chest without any intervening clothing[4].

The rules to be observed in the practice of auscultation, in health and disease, may be here introduced.

In auscultation, as in percussion, corresponding situations on the two sides of the chest are to be explored successively, and compared. When the stethoscope is used, the pectoral extremity must be applied on each side with the same degree of pressure; this is especially essential in the comparison of vocal sounds. In immediate auscultation, the ear is to be applied with a certain degree of force, and a thin layer of clothing does not interfere materially with the perception of auscultatory sounds. The ear not applied to the chest may or may not be closed by the finger in listening to the respiratory sounds; it should be closed in listening to the vocal sounds, in order to prevent confusion from attention to the voice from the patient's mouth. In immediate auscultation, whenever practised, the auscultator should take a position which will not interfere with the sense of hearing, and not occasion a feeling of discomfort. These difficulties are in the way of auscultating with the body bent forward; the sense of hearing is dulled by the gravitation of blood to the head, and the position cannot be maintained without discomfort. The person examined, if practicable, should be sitting, and the best position for the auscultator is that of

---

4 The stethoscopes made by Tiemann & Co. are reliable.

kneeling on one knee, and lowering, if necessary, the body, so that the head may be kept upright. These points need not be observed if the binaural stethoscope be used.

When listening to respiratory sounds, it is generally desirable that the person examined should breathe with somewhat greater force than in ordinary breathing; but it is important that the normal rhythm of respiration should be unchanged. Persons when requested to breathe with increased force are apt to err in breathing violently, and sometimes too slowly. The readiest mode of obtaining what is desired, is for the examiner to illustrate it by his own breathing. A complete expiration is important in order to secure a satisfactory inspiration. It should, therefore, be made clear, by explanation and illustration, that each expiration should be finished before the following inspiration.

The ability to abstract the mind from thoughts and other sounds than those to which the attention is to be directed, is essential to success in auscultation. All persons do not possess equally this ability, and herein is an explanation in part of the fact that all are not alike successful. To develop and cultivate by practice the power of concentration, is an object which the student should keep in view. Generally, at first, complete stillness in the room is indispensable for the study of auscultatory sounds; with practice, however, in concentrating the attention, this becomes less and less essential.

The study of auscultation in health embraces the following:—

1. The sounds produced by respiration as heard over the larynx and trachea, or the ***normal laryngeal and tracheal respiration.***

2. The sounds beard over the chest in the acts of respiration. These sounds, coming chiefly from the air-vesicles, constitute what is called the ***normal vesicular murmur.***

3. The resonance, as heard over the chest, and the vibration or thrill produced by the loud voice, or the ***normal vocal resonance and fremilus.***

4. The sounds, as heard over the chest with the whispered voice, or, inasmuch as these sounds are conducted chiefly by the air in the bronchial tubes, the ***normal bronchial whisper.***

Those four normal signs will be considered in the foregoing order.

Normal Laryngeal and Tracheal Respiration.

For all practical purposes the laryngeal and the tracheal respiration may be considered to be identical, that is, the shades of difference between the sounds in these two situations are not of importance as regards the application to physical diagnosis. The laryngeal respiration is more readily studied than the tracheal, and, for the study of both, the stethoscope is necessary.

Applying the stethoscope over the side of the larynx, the person examined breathing with some increase of force, but without any alteration in rhythm, a sound is heard with each of the two acts of respiration. The inspiratory and the expiratory sound, studied separately and contrasted with each other, have the following characters relating to intensity, pitch, quality, duration, and rhythm: The inspiratory sound is of variable intensity. In ordinary breathing it varies much in different persons, and in different acts of breathing in the same person. It is always considerably intense in forced breathing. The pitch is high when compared with the inspiratory sound as heard over the chest. The quality of the sound is well defined by the word tubular; the sound at once suggests a current of air through a tube. The duration of the sound is from the beginning to nearly, not quite, the end of the inspiratory act. The characters of the inspiratory sound, thus, are more or less intensity, a high pitch, a tubular quality, and a duration a little less than that of the act of inspiration.

An expiratory sound is always heard with forced breathing. As regards duration, it is as long as, or longer than, the sound of inspiration. In general it is more intense than the sound of inspiration. The pitch is higher than that of the inspiratory sound. The quality is the same as that of the inspiratory sound, namely, tubular.

Repeating the characters distinctive of the normal laryngeal respiration, they are as follows: The inspiratory sound is of variable intensity, high in pitch, and tubular in quality. The expiratory sound is as long as, or longer than, the inspiratory sound; it is higher in pitch, and usually more intense, Owing to the inspiratory sound not continuing quite to the end of the inspiratory act, there is a very short interval between the two sounds. In this latter point consists the only variation between the rhythm of the acts of breathing and that of the sounds.

The foregoing characters should not only be verified by the student, but he should become so familiar with them by practice that it requires no effort of the mind to recollect them. It will be seen hereafter that these characters of the normal laryngeal respiration are precisely those which distinguish an important morbid physical sign, namely, the bronchial or tubular respiration.

Normal Vesicular Murmur.

This is the name usually given to the respiratory sounds heard over the different regions of the chest. These sounds should be studied with the ear applied directly to the chest (immediate auscultation), as well as with the stethoscope. In commencing the study, the middle of the anterior surface of the chest on the right side, to avoid the sounds of the heart, or, still better, the posterior aspect below the scapula on either side, should be selected. The person examined should breathe somewhat more forcibly than in ordinary breathing, but not violently or quickly, nor too slowly, the normal rhythm being unchanged. Children are better than adults for this study, owing to the greater intensity of the murmur in early life.

The characters which belong to the inspiratory and the expiratory sound in the normal vesicular murmur are as follows: The inspiratory sound is of variable intensity. There is a wide variation in different healthy persons. In some persons it is so feeble as scarcely to be appreciable even with the binaural stethoscope. The pitch of the sound, compared with the inspiratory sound in the normal laryngeal or tracheal respiration, is notably low. The quality of the sound is peculiar; no distinct idea of the quality can be formed by any comparison. The name used to designate the quality is ***vesicular,*** this name only denoting that the air vesicles are in some way concerned in the production of the sound. This vesicular quality must be impressed upon the perception and memory by direct observation. The duration of the inspiratory sound is from the beginning to the end of the inspiratory act.

An expiratory sound is not always, although generally, appreciable. It is much less intense than the sound of inspiration. It is notably lower in pitch than the sound of inspiration. The quality of the sound is neither vesicular nor tubular. It may be called simply a blowing sound, and may be imitated by blowing with the mouth partially opened. The duration is much shorter than that of the inspiratory sound.

The characters, thus, which distinguish the normal vesicular murmur are, an inspiratory sound variable in intensity, low in pitch, and vesicular in quality; an expiratory sound less intense than the inspiratory, still lower in pitch, non-vesicular and non-tubular, or simply blowing; the inspiratory sound continuing from the beginning to the end of the inspiratory act, and the expiratory sound beginning with the expiratory act but ending before this act is completed, its duration, relatively to the inspiratory sound, being variable, but averaging about a fifth. The inspiratory sound continuing to the end of inspiration, and the expiratory sound beginning with the act of expiration, it follows that there is no interval between the two sounds. It is to be remarked that an interval is not infrequently produced by the person examined holding the breath after inspiration is completed. This variation in the rhythm of the acts, of course, produces a corresponding variation in sounds of breathing.

The student should verify these characters, compare them with the characters of the normal laryngeal respiration, and become practically familiar with the differential points. He should then proceed to study the normal vesicular murmur in the different regions of the chest. The murmur will be found to present variations in the different regions on the same side, and in the corresponding regions on the two sides of the chest. The variations, within the range of health, in the latter are especially important. The following account of the murmur in the different regions embodies the results of a series of recorded examinations of healthy persons.

Right and Left Infra-clavicular Region.—The murmur in this region, on either side, differs more or less from the murmur as heard in the anterior regions below, or in the infra-scapular region. The vesicular quality in the inspiration is less marked. The pitch is higher. The expiratory sound is longer, less feeble, and higher in pitch. The difference between the two sides in this region is especially important with reference to diagnosis. The intensity of the inspiratory sound is almost invariably greater on the left side. Its vesicular quality is more marked, and the pitch is lower. *Per contra,* the inspiratory sound on the right side, in this region, is less intense, less vesicular, and higher in pitch than the inspiratory sound on the left side. In forced breathing the intensity of the murmur is increased more on the left than on the right side. The expiratory sound is sometimes wanting on the left, when it is heard on the right side. On the right side, the expiratory sound is longer than on the left side. It may be prolonged on the right side to nearly or quite the length of the inspiratory sound. Sometimes on the right side the pitch of the expiratory is higher than that of the inspiratory on the same side, and it may have a tubular quality. A rare peculiarity is a prolonged, high, tubular expiratory sound on both sides, analogous to the laryngeal or tracheal expiration. When this is the case, the pitch of the expiratory sound is higher on the left than on the right side.

These several modifications of the respiratory murmur in the infra-clavicular region are marked in proportion as the sounds are studied near the sternum, that is, over the site of the primary bronchi. The respiratory murmur in this situation has been called the normal bronchial respiration, from its resemblance to the morbid sign so named. It may be more properly called a vesiculo-tubular, or the normal broncho-vesicular respiration, the characters being those of the morbid sign which, under the latter name, will be described in the next chapter.

In the diagnosis of diseases, especially of phthisis, due allowance must be made for the points of disparity which exist normally between the two sides of the chest in the infra-clavicular region. Without a practical knowledge of these points of disparity, error in diagnosis can hardly be avoided.

Right and Left Scapular Region.—As compared with the infra-clavicular region, the respiratory murmur heard over the scapula on either side is feeble, and the vesicular quality is less marked. The inspiratory sound is generally weaker and the pitch higher on the right than on the left side. The expiratory sound is more constantly heard on the right than on the left side. It may be prolonged on the right side, and is sometimes higher in pitch than the inspiratory sound. Compared with the left side, the murmur on the right, in this region, thus may have vesiculo-tubular or broncho-vesicular characters more or less marked.

Right and Left Inter scapular Region.—In the upper and middle portions of this region, the normal characters are the same as in the sterno-clavicular portion of infra-clavicular region. The same points of disparity between the two sides are more or less marked here as they are anteriorly over the site of the primary bronchi.

Right and Left Infra-scapular Region.—The intensity of the murmur is greater than over the scapular region. In most persons there is no notable disparity between the two sides; when a disparity exists, the intensity is greater and the pitch lower on the left side. A prolonged, high pitched, bronchial expiratory sound is sometimes transmitted below the scapula on the right side.

Right and Left Mammary and Infra-mammary Regions.—The inspiratory sound in these regions is less intense than in the infra-clavicular region; the vesicular quality is more marked, and the pitch is lower. An expiratory sound is often wanting.

Right and Left Axillary and Infra-axillary Regions.—The inspiratory sound in these regions is as intense as in any portion of the chest. The intensity is less in the infra-axillary than in the axillary region, and the pitch is lower. In some persons the murmur on the two sides presents no disparity, but in other persons the vesicular quality is somewhat more marked and the pitch is lower on the left than on the right side. An expiratory sound is oftener heard than in the mammary and infra-mammary regions.

Normal Vocal Resonance.

Laryngeal and Tracheal Voice.—It will prepare the student for the appreciation of the distinctive characters of the morbid signs pertaining to the voice, to study the vocal signs over the larynx and trachea. Applying the stethoscope either over the broad surface of the thyroid cartilage, or just above the sternal notch, and requesting the person examined to count with a moderate intensity of voice, the auscultator perceives a strong resonance with a sensation of concussion or shock, and a sense of vibration, thrill, or fremitus. The voice seems to be concentrated and near the ear. Sometimes the articulated words are transmitted so as to be heard more or less distinctly. The laryngeal or tracheal voice, thus (laryngophony, tracheophony), embraces different elements, namely, 1st, the vocal resonance; 2d, the concentration and nearness to the ear; 3d, the vibration, thrill, or fremitus; and 4th, the transmission of the speech, the latter corresponding to pectoriloquy. These different elements will be found to enter into the distinctive characters of morbid vocal signs.

The sounds heard over the larynx and trachea when words are spoken in a whisper should be studied, inasmuch as important morbid signs relate to the whispered voice. Whispered words occasion little or no shock or thrill, but an intense, high pitched, tubular sound, with a sensation as if a current of air were directed into the ear through the stethoscope. This sound corresponds to the sound of expiration in laryngeal or tracheal respiration; the two sounds are, in fact, identical if, as is the case with some exceptions, the person whisper with the expiratory breath. Articulated words are transmitted with more or less distinctness, corresponding with the morbid sign called whispering pectoriloquy.

Normal Thoracic Vocal Resonance and Fremitus.—The vocal resonance over the chest is to be studied both by means of the stethoscope and by immediate auscultation. When the latter is employed, the ear not applied to the chest should be closed, in order to exclude the entrance of sound from the mouth of the person examined. When the stethoscope is employed, care must be taken, in making a comparison between the two sides of the chest, or between different regions on the same side, that the pectoral extremity of the instrument be pressed with an equal amount of force against the chest. The intensity with which the vocal resonance is transmitted, is much affected by the degree of pressure with the stethoscope.

The situations in which the student should commence the study of the normal vocal resonance are those selected for beginning the study of the normal vesicular murmur, namely, the middle of the anterior aspect of the chest on the right side, and below the scapula behind.

With the stethoscope or the ear directly applied in the situations just named, the person examined should be requested to count one, two, three, in a uniform tune, and with moderate force. The examiner should himself pronounce these numerals, in order to show the manner of counting. This is far better than asking a question and studying the resonance during the answer of the person examined. The objection to the latter mode is, the attention of the examiner is divided between the characters of the thoracic resonance and the idea conveyed by the answer. The characters of the vocal resonance in these situations are as follows:—

The voice is heard with an intensity which varies very much in different persons; in some the resonance is feeble, and it may be almost inappreciable, while in others it is quite intense. The intensity depends greatly on the loudness and lowness in pitch of the voice of the person examined. The resonance is notably weaker in women than in men. It is rarely attended with a sense of concussion or shock. It is diffused; that is, it does not seem to be concentrated, like the tracheal or laryngeal vocal resonance. It evidently conies from a certain distance; that is, the sound does not seem to be near the ear. This latter character is distinctly appreciable, and is highly distinctive of the normal resonance as compared with a morbid vocal sign (bronchophony). The resonance is accompanied by a sense of vibration, thrill, or fremitus, the intensity of which, like the resonance, varies much in different persons. This fremitus is properly not an acoustic but a tactile sign. The normal vocal fremitus, together with its abnormal modifications, belongs to the method of physical exploration called palpation. It is, however, appreciated by the ear as well as by the touch, and may be studied in the practice of auscultation. The student should practically distinguish from each other, and study separately, the vocal resonance and vocal fremitus.

From the foregoing characters the normal vocal resonance may be defined as, diffused, distant, variable in intensity, and accompanied with more or less vibration, thrill, or fremitus.

Having become practically familiar with these characters of the normal vocal resonance in the situations in which they are first to be studied, the next object of study relates to the normal variations in the different regions on the same side of the chest, and in corresponding regions on the two sides. In giving an account of these variations, based on a series of recorded examinations in healthy persons, the different regions will be considered in the same order; is in the study of the variations of the respiratory sounds (*vide* p. 78 *et seq.*).

Infra-clavicular Region.—The vocal resonance in this region on either side is more intense than in the anterior regions below, the intensity, however, in different persons being very variable; irrespective of intensity, it is less diffused, nearer the ear, and the pitch is somewhat higher. These latter variations are marked chiefly in the sterno-clavicular extremity of the region, that is, over the site of the primary bronchi. In some persons the concentration, nearness to the ear and elevation of pitch, especially on the right side, are such as to approximate the normal resonance to the morbid sign called bronchophony. The characters of this sign will be considered in the next chapter; but it is important to know that exceptionally these characters may be, in a measure, illustrated in health in the infra-clavicular region. The resonance might then be termed normal bronchophony.

A comparison of the resonance in the region on the right and on the left side always shows a disparity. The resonance on the right side is invariably greater. The degree of difference between the two sides varies in different persons. The resonance may be more or less marked on the right and nearly wanting on the left side. Allowance is to be made for the points of normal disparity between the two sides in the diagnosis of disease; hence the student must become practically familiar with them.

The vocal vibration or fremitus varies fully as much as the vocal resonance in different persons. Its intensity is not always proportionate to that of the resonance; that is, the resonance may be comparatively weak when the fremitus is strong, and *vice versa.* The fremitus, like the resonance, is always greater on the right than on the left side, the disparity, like that of the resonance, varying considerably in different persons.

Scapular Region.—The resonance in this region is notably less intense than in the infra-clavicular region. It is also more diffused and distant. The intensity is always greater on the right side. These statements are alike applicable to the vocal fremitus.

Inter scapular Region.—The intensity of the resonance here is nearly or quite as great as in the sterno-clavicular extremity of the infra-clavicular region. The resonance has in some persons in this region the characters of bronchophony. The intensity is always greater on the right side. The fremitus is more or less marked, and always more marked on the right than on the left side.

Infra-scapular Region.—As a rule the resonance in this region is stronger than over the scapula. It is always characterized by diffusion and distance. As in all the regions it varies much in different persons, and is stronger on the right than on the left side. These statements are also applicable to fremitus.

Mammary and Infra-mammary Regions.—The resonance is notably less than at the summit of the chest. The characters of bronchophony are never present. The intensity is greater on the right side. The same is true of fremitus.

Axillary and Infra-axillary Regions.—The resonance in these regions, and especially in the axillary region, is greater than over the mammary and infra-mammary regions. It is, of course, stronger on the right side. The characters, as contrasted with those of bronchophony, namely, distance and diffusion, are marked. Fremitus is more or less marked, and, of course, more marked on the right than on the left side.

Normal Bronchial Whisper.

Prior to the publication of the author's work on the "Physical Exploration of the Chest" in 1856, signs in health and disease relating to the whispered voice had received but little attention. In that work, and more fully in the second edition, published in 1866, a series of signs accompanying whispered words were described and named. As a point of departure for the study of the morbid signs thus obtained, of course, the signs in health must first be studied. The sounds which are heard over different parts of the chest in health I have embraced under the name, the normal bronchial whisper. The pertinency of this name is derived from the fact that the conduction of the sound produced by the whispered voice must be chiefly by the air contained in the bronchial tubes. The sound heard over the trachea and larynx may be distinguished as the laryngeal or tracheal whisper, the characters of which have been already stated (*vide* page 82).

It will facilitate the study of the normal bronchial whisper, as well as of the morbid signs. to consider that the characters of the sounds produced with the whispered voice, are identical with those produced by the act of expiration, in all respects, save intensity. Whispered words are produced, as a rule, by an act of expiration, the sounds being more intense generally than those which accompany even forced breathing. Curiously enough, there are exceptions to this rule. Some persons insist upon whispering with the act of inspiration, and there are some persons who have never acquired the ability to whisper, It will be at once evident that the pitch and quality of sounds produced by whispered words with the act of expiration, must be the same as those of the sounds of expiration in breathing.

Selecting for beginning the study of the normal bronchial whisper the same situations as in commencing the study of the normal respiratory murmur, and the normal vocal resonance, namely, the middle of the chest in front, on the right side, and the infra-scapular region behind, with the whispered voice in these situations is heard, in most persons, a feeble, low-pitched, blowing sound, these characters corresponding to those of the expiratory sound in forced breathing. The normal bronchial whisper in these situations is not in all persons appreciable.

In the infra-clavicular region, the bronchial whisper is heard, with variable intensity, in most persons. It is somewhat higher in pitch than the whisper below this region. It is louder and higher in the sterno-clavicular than in the acromial extremity. In the former situation it has not infrequently a tubular quality. It is louder on the right than on the left side of the chest. It is sometimes heard on the right when

tions correspond to those of the sound with expiration in the infra-clavicular region (*vide* page 79). Occasionally whispered words are partly transmitted, constituting incomplete whispering pectoriloquy.

In the scapular region the bronchial whisper is not infrequently wanting. It may be present on the right and not on the left side, and, if present on both sides, it is always louder on the right side.

In the inter-scapular region, as a rule, it is nearly or quite as marked as over the site of the primary bronchi in front. The pitch is more or less high, and has a tubular quality. It is louder on the right and higher in pitch on the left side, and in this situation there may be incomplete pectoriloquy.

In the infra-scapular region, it is not infrequently wanting. When present, it is generally feeble, the pitch being low and the quality non-tubular or blowing. It is oftener wanting on the left than on the right side, and, if present on both sides, it is louder on the right side.

In the mammary and infra-mammary regions it is not infrequently wanting, and the statements just made with reference to the infra-scapular region are alike applicable to these, as also, to the axillary and infra-axillary regions.

CHAPTER V.
AUSCULTATION IN DISEASE.

The respiratory signs of disease:—Abnormal modifications of the normal respiratory sounds:—Increased vesicular murmur—Diminished vesicular murmur—Suppressed respiratory sound—Bronchial or tubular respiration—Broncho-vesicular respiration—Cavernous respiration—Bronchocavernous respiration—Amphoric respiration—Shortened inspiration—Prolonged expiration—Interrupted respiration. Adventitious respiratory sounds or rales:—Laryngeal and tracheal rale—Moist bronchial rales, coarse, fine, and subcrepitant—Vesicular or crepitant rale—Cavernous or gurgling rule—Pleural friction rales, metallic tinkling and splashing. Indeterminate rales—The vocal signs of disease:—Bronchophony—Whispering bronchophony—Ægophony—Increased vocal resonance—Increased bronchial whisper—Cavernous whisper—Pectoriloquy—Amphoric voice or echo—Diminished and suppressed vocal resonance—Diminished and suppressed vocal fremitis—Metallic tinkling. Signs obtained by acts of coughing or tussive signs.

THE importance of becoming perfectly familiar with the signs of health before entering upon the study of morbid signs, cannot be too strongly enforced. The auscultatory signs of disease, which are to be considered in this chapter, should not be studied until the student has made himself complete master of all the characters belonging to the normal signs obtained by auscultation.

Auscultation in disease embraces the signs produced by respiration, by the voice, and by acts of coughing. The respiratory signs will be first considered.

The Respiratory Signs of Disease.

The signs produced by respiration may be classified as follows: 1st. Those which are abnormal modifications of the normal respiratory sounds. 2d. Those which have no analogues in health, being entirely new or adventitious sounds. The latter are embraced under the name *rales.*

Abnormal Modifications of the Normal Respiratory Sounds.

In order to appreciate the distinctive characters of the signs embraced in this class, the characters which distinguish the normal vesicular murmur must be kept in mind. The abnormal modifications which characterize these morbid signs relate to intensity, pitch, and quality of sound, together with certain alterations in rhythm. Eleven distinct modifications or signs are included under this heading, namely: 1. Increased vesicular murmur; 2. Diminished vesicular murmur; 3. Suppression of respiratory sound; 4. Bronchial or tubular respiration; 5. Broncho-vesicular respiration; 6. Cavernous respiration; 7. Broncho-cavernous respiration; 8. Amphoric respiration; 9. Shortened inspiration; 10. Prolonged expiration; and, 11. Interrupted inspiration or expiration.

These signs are to be studied, first, with reference to their distinctive characters severally, each being contrasted, as respects these characters, with the other morbid respiratory signs as well as with the normal vesicular murmur; and, second, with reference to the morbid physical conditions which they represent, that is, the diagnostic significance which belongs to each.

Increased Vesicular Murmur.—This sign has but a single distinctive character, namely, increase of intensity. The murmur is abnormally loud, the characters of the normal vesicular murmur being in other respects not materially changed, that is, the pitch is low and the quality vesicular as in health. Now, it has been seen (***vide*** page 77) that the intensity of the healthy murmur varies much in different persons; there is no ideal standard of normal intensity by reference to which an abnormal increase is to be determined. Yet, the increase under certain conditions of disease a such that the fact is sufficiently evident. It occurs on the healthy side of the chest when the respiratory function on the other side is annulled or much compromised by disease. This takes place in cases of pleurisy with large effusion, pneumonia, especially if more than one lobe ho affected, obstruction of one of the primary bronchi, and pneumothorax. The sign does not possess great diagnostic importance, inasmuch as the nature and extent of the disease are determined by the signs obtained on the affected side.

The sign has been called ***supplementary*** and ***puerile*** respiration.

If the murmur be much intensified, it may possibly be mistaken for other morbid signs, namely, bronchial or broncho-vesicular respiration. This error, however, can never he made if the distinctive characters of these signs relating to pitch and quality have been correctly studied.

Diminished Vesicular Murmur.—The intensity of the vesicular murmur may be on the one hand diminished, when it is evident that in other respects there is no material change, and the murmur, on the other hand, may become so feeble that characters aside from the intensity are not determinable. From the latter fact it follows that the murmur must sometimes be considered as only weakened, when, were the diminished intensity not as great, morbid changes in pitch and quality might be appreciable.

The murmur is more or less weakened in cases of dilatation of the air cells, or vesicular emphysema, the sign, in these cases, being often accompanied by changes in rhythm, namely, a shortened inspiration and a prolonged expiration. Simple weakness of the murmur may also be incident to partial blocking of the air vesicles with blood or serum in cases of pulmonary extravasation and œdema. A deficient expansion of the chest, either on one side or on both sides, occasions weakness of the respiratory murmur. Deficient expansion of one side, or of both sides, may be caused by paralysis, bi-lateral, or unilateral, of the costal muscles. A similar effect is caused by paralysis of the diaphragm. The incomplete descent of the diaphragm from pain, as in peritonitis, or from mechanical obstacles as in peritoneal dropsy, pregnancy, and abdominal tumors, weakens the respiratory murmur, the increased action of the costal muscles not being fully compensatory. Unilateral deficiency of expansion of the chest is caused by pain in intercostal neuralgia, pleurodynia, acute pleurisy, and pneumonia; it is also caused by the presence of a stratum of liquid, air, or a thick layer of lymph between the lung and the chest-wall in pleurisy, hydrothorax and pneumothorax. Swelling of the bronchial mucous membrane in bronchitis affecting the larger tubes, must diminish somewhat the intensity of the murmur. In primary bronchitis, the murmur is diminished on both sides. In bronchitis affecting the smaller tubes, the murmur is greatly diminished, if not suppressed, on both sides. Incomplete obstruction of bronchial tubes from the presence of mucus, serum, blood, or pus, has this effect over an area corresponding to the size of the tubes obstructed. Spasm of the bronchial muscular fibres in paroxysms of asthma, diminishes, if it does not suppress, murmur on both sides. Another cause of diminution, unilateral, or within a limited space on one side, is the pressure of a tumor on bronchial tubes, as in cases of aneurism. A permanent contraction or stricture of bronchial tubes is another cause. Not infrequently the pressure of an aneurismal tumor or an enlarged bronchial gland on a primary bronchus, occasions notable weakness of the murmur over the whole of one side; and the pressure of a tumor on the trachea weakens the murmur, more or less, on both sides. A foreign body in one of the primary bronchi weakens it on one side. Diminution of the calibre of the trachea or larynx from morbid growths, the presence of foreign bodies, fibrinous exudation, accumulations of mucus, sub-mucous infiltration, spasm of the laryngeal muscles, and swelling of the mucous membrane, weakens, in proportion to the amount of obstruction, the murmur on both sides without any material change in its quality and pitch.

Weakened murmur at the summit of the chest, without other appreciable abnormal characters, occurs in some cases of phthisis, due to obstructed bronchial tubes from coexisting circumscribed bronchitis, or to deficient superior costal movements of the chest, as well as to the presence of exudation in air vesicles.

Diminished intensity of the vesicular murmur is thus seen to be a respiratory sign entering into the diagnosis of a considerable number of diseases, namely, emphysema, paralysis affecting the respiratory muscles, asthma, abdominal affections interfering with the diaphragmatic movements, intercostal neuralgia, pleurodynia, pneumothorax, acute pleurisy, pneumonia, hydrothorax, bronchitis, asthma, aneurismal and other tumours, permanent constriction or stricture of bronchial tubes, laryngitis, œdema of the glottis, spasm of the glottis, the various lesions which occasion obstruction of the larynx or trachea, and phthisis.

In determining a slight abnormal weakness of the respiratory murmur at the summit of the chest on the right side, the normal disparity between the two sides in this situation is to be borne in mind. The vesicular murmur is normally less intense on the right than on the left side.

This sign occurring in so man diseases, it is obvious that, taken alone, that is, independently of other signs, it has not any special diagnostic significance. It is, however, often of value in diagnosis, when taken in connection with other signs. It is chiefly useful when it exists either over the whole or in a part of the chest on one side.

Suppressed Respiratory Sound.—This sign is easily defined, namely, absence of all respiratory sound, as the name signifies. It cannot, of course, have any characters relating to intensity, pitch, and quality.

Suppression of respiratory sound represents the same physical conditions as diminished vesicular murmur; the physical conditions represented by the latter sign, existing in a greater degree, occasion absence of all sound. It suffices, therefore, to recapitulate the various conditions and diseases in connection with which the murmur may either be diminished or suppressed. Suppression over portions of the chest may be due to dilatation of the air-cells in cases of empyema. It occurs from the exclusion of air from the vesicles by the presence of blood and serum in cases of pulmonary extravasation and œdema. Respiratory sound is sometimes wanting over lung solidified in cases of pneumonia and phthisis. Paralysis of the muscles concerned in respiration may possibly involve feebleness of the respiratory acts sufficiently to render the murmur inappreciable. In intercostal neuralgia, pleurodynia, acute pleurisy, and pneumonia, the movements of the affected side may be so much restricted as to abolish the murmur. In pleurisy with much effusion, empyema, hydrothorax, pneumothorax, the murmur is suppressed over either a part or the whole of the affected side, the extent of the suppression corresponding to the quantity of serum, pus, or air within the pleural cavity. Swelling of the mucous membrane in cases of bronchitis affecting the larger bronchial tubes is never sufficient to suppress the murmur, hut plugging of more or less of the tubes with mucus or other morbid products may have this effect. In cases of bronchitis, the murmur is sometimes found to have disappeared over a certain area, and to return after an act of expectoration. In bronchitis affecting the smaller tubes, suppression of the murmur is not infrequent. It occurs from spasm of the bronchial muscular fibres in cases of asthma. The pressure of a tumour, morbid growths, or deposits upon bronchi within the lungs, may abolish respiratory sound over a portion of the chest, and permanent stricture or obliteration of bronchial tubes have this effect. Respiratory sound may be suppressed over the whole of one side from the pressure of an aneurismal or some other tumour upon one of the primary bronchi. If the tumour press upon the trachea, the obstruction may be sufficient to suppress the murmur on both sides. A foreign body lodged in a primary bronchus may suppress the murmur on one side, and, lodged in the larynx or trachea, the murmur may be suppressed on both sides. The different affections of the larynx and trachea which, in proportion to the amount of obstruction, weaken the murmur, may render it inappreciable.

Bronchial or Tubular Respiration.—The analogue of this sign is the normal laryngeal or tracheal respiration (***vide*** page 74). The characters which distinguish the latter normal sign from the normal vesicular murmur, are those which are distinctive of the bronchial or tubular respiration. These characters, relating to the inspiratory and the expiratory sound, are as follows: The inspiratory sound is of variable intensity. Intensity does not enter into the distinctive characters of this sign; the sound may be either louder or weaker than the inspiratory sound in health. The pitch of the inspiratory sound is high. The quality is expressed by the term tubular; it is like the sound produced by blowing through a tube, this quality taking the place of that expressed by the term vesicular in the normal respiration. The expiratory sound is prolonged; it is as long as, or longer than, the sound of expiration, and is usually louder. The pitch is still higher than that of the inspiratory sound. The quality, like that of the inspiratory sound, is tubular, this quality taking the place of the simple blowing quality of the expiratory sound in the normal vesicular murmur. With the normal rhythm of the respiratory acts, there is a very brief interval between the sounds of inspiration and expiration, due to the fact that the inspiratory sound ends a little before the end of the inspiratory act.

The morbid physical condition represented by this important sign is either complete or considerable solidification of lung. Whenever the chest is auscultated over lung solidified, if there be not absence of respiratory sound, the sound is tubular. This significance renders the sign of diagnostic value in the diseases which involve solidification. The sign ***per se*** denotes simply this morbid physical condition; the particular disease which exists is ascertained by means of the associated signs and the symptoms.

Solidification of lung is incident to several different diseases. In lobar or vesicular pneumonia, it is due to a fibrinous exudation within the air vesicles. In phthisis it is caused by an exudation in the same situation. In chronic or fibroid pneumonia the lung is solidified by an interstitial growth. The compression of lung from either pleuritic effusion, an accumulation of air in the pleural cavity, or the pressure of a tumor, causes solidification by condensation. Collapse of pulmonary lobules also solidities by condensation. Coagulation of blood within the air vesicles (hemorrhagic infarctus), and cancerous infiltration or growth, are other causes of solidification. In these different affections, if the solidification be complete or considerable, this sign is usually present; it is always present if there be not suppression of respiratory sound.

It is sometimes the case that either the inspiratory or the expiratory sound is wanting. The characters of the sign suffice for its recognition if either the inspiratory or the expiratory sound be alone present; the pitch and the quality are distinctive. Both sounds are often so intense that they are diffused more or loss without the limits of the solidified portion of lung. The expiratory sound, being more intense than the inspiratory, is transmitted further than the latter. This explains the conjunction sometimes of a vesicular inspiration with a tubular expiration; and a cavernous inspiration may be conjoined with a tubular expiration, showing the proximity of solidified lung in the former case to healthy lung, and, in the latter case, to a pulmonary cavity.

The sound may seem near the ear or to come from a certain distance. The latter is appreciable in some cases of large pleuritic effusion; the tubular respiration is more or less distant, and it is sometimes diffused over the whole of the side which is filled with liquid.

Broncho-vesicular Respiration.—This name was introduced by me in 1856 to denote the combination, in varying proportions, of the characters of the bronchial or tubular, and of the normal vesicular respiration. The name expresses such a combination.

The sign represents the different degrees of solidification of lung, between an amount so slight as to occasion only the smallest appreciable modification of the respiratory sound, and an amount so great as to approximate closely to the degree giving rise to bronchial or tubular respiration. In other words, all the gradations of respiratory modifications, caused by incomplete or an inconsiderable solidification, which fall short of bronchial or tubular respiration, are embraced under the name broncho-vesicular. The gradations correspond to the amount of solidification, that is, they show the solidification to be either very slight, slight, moderate, or nearly sufficient to be considered as considerable or complete. The sign is therefore important as evidence, first, of the existence of solidification, and second, of the degree of solidification.

Analyzing this sign, the most distinctive feature is the combination of the vesicular and the tubular quality in the inspiratory sound. These two qualities ma be combined in variable proportions. The pitch of the sound is raised in proportion as the tubular predominates over the vesicular quality. The expiratory sound is more or less prolonged, tubular in quality, and the pitch is raised. The prolongation of this sound, its tubular quality, and the highness of pitch, are proportionate to the predominance of the tubular over the vesicular quality in the inspiratory sound. If the solidification of lung be slight, the characters of the normal vesicular respiration predominate; that is, the inspiratory sound has but a small proportion of the tubular quality, and is but little raised in pitch, the expiratory sound being not much prolonged, its tubularity not marked, the pitch not high. If, on the other hand, the solidification of lung be almost enough to give a bronchial respiration, the inspiratory sound has only a little vesicular quality, the tubular quality predominating, the pitch proportionately raised; and the expiratory sound is prolonged, tubular, and high, nearly to the same extent as in the bronchial respiration. The less the solidification the more the characters of the normal vesicular predominate over those of the bronchial respiration, and, ***per contra,*** the greater the solidification the more the characters of the bronchial predominate over those of the normal vesicular respiration. Daily auscultation in a case of lobar pneumonia during the stage of resolution affords an opportunity to Study all the gradations of this sign. After resolution has made some progress, the inspiratory sound is no longer purely tubular, but the ear appreciates a little admixture of the vesicular quality and the pitch is slightly lowered. As the resolution goes on, the vesicular quality increases, the pitch is correspondingly lowered, until, at length, no tubularity remains, and the pitch becomes normal. Meanwhile, as the vesicular quality increases in the inspiratory sound, the expiratory sound is less and less prolonged, high and tubular, until it becomes, as in health, short, low, and blowing.

The broncho-vesicular respiration is an important diagnostic sign in all the affections which involve partial solidification of lung. In lobar pneumonia, as just stated, it denotes the progress made from day to day in resolution. It is found also in an earlier stage, before the solidification is sufficient to give rise to a purely bronchial respiration. It is a valuable sign in phthisis, affording evidence, not only of the fact of solidification, but of its degree and extent. The sign enters into the diagnosis of interstitial pneumonia, hemorrhagic infarctus, condensation of lung from the pressure of either liquid, air, or a tumor, and from collapse of pulmonary lobules. It may be stated, with respect to this sign, that it is always present, if the lung be partially solidified, provided there be not either suppression of respiratory sound, or such a degree of feebleness that the distinctive characters are undeterminable. As with the bronchial respiration, so with the broncho-vesicular, either the inspiratory or the expiratory sound may be wanting. The characters of the sign are then to be determined as they are manifested in the sound which is present, namely, the combination of the vesicular and the tubular quality, with more or less elevation of pitch, if only an inspiratory sound be heard, and the amount of prolongation, tubularity, and elevation of pitch, if there be only an expiratory sound.

In determining the presence of this morbid sign, at the summit of the chest on the right side, it is to be borne in mind that the respiratory murmur on this side has, in health, as compared with the respiratory murmur at the summit on the left side, more or less of the characters of the broncho-vesicular respiration (***vide*** Normal Broncho-vesicular Respiration, page 79).

Cavernous Respiration.—The modifications which constitute the distinctive characters of this sign, are produced by the entrance of air into a cavity with the act of inspiration, and its exit from the cavity with the act of expiration. This passage of air into and from a cavity can only take place where the walls of the cavity collapse more or less in expiration and expand in inspiration. Pulmonary cavities occur chiefly in cases of phthisis. They occur, but with comparative infrequency, as a result of circumscribed abscess and gangrene of lung.

A well-marked cavernous respiration has characters which are highly distinctive when this sign is contrasted, on the one hand, with either the bronchial or broncho-vesicular respiration, and, on the other hand, with the normal vesicular murmur. These distinctive characters relate both to the inspiratory and the expiratory sound. The inspiratory sound is neither vesicular nor tabular in quality, and the pitch is low as compared with the bronchial respiration. As regards quality, we may say of it, as of the expiratory sound in the normal vesicular respiration, it is simply a blowing sound. The expiratory sound has the same quality as the inspiratory, and it is lower in pitch. Its duration is variable. The intensity of both the inspiratory and the expiratory sound varies; intensity does not enter into the distinctive characters of this sign more than into those of the bronchial and the broncho-vesicular respiration. These distinctive characters of the cavernous respiration, as regards pitch and quality, especially of the expiratory sound, were first pointed out by me in 1852.[5] Prior to this date the bronchial and the cavernous respiration were considered as having identical characters, or, at all events, as not distinguishable from each other. With a practical knowledge of the foregoing characters distinctive of the cavernous respiration, there is no difficulty in discriminating this sign from the bronchia respiration. The sign is more likely to he confounded with the normal vesicular murmur, inasmuch as it differs from the latter only in the absence, in the inspiratory sound, of the vesicular quality. Against this error the student is to be cautioned. It is most likely to be made when the inspiratory sound is much weakened, and, consequently, the vesicular quality is less distinctly appreciable than when the sound is more or less intense.

A cavernous respiration is limited to a space more or loss circumscribed, the area corresponding to the site and the size of the cavity. Occurring, for the most part, in cases of phthisis, it is much oftener found at the summit than elsewhere over the chest. It is not constantly found where there is a cavity with flaccid walls. It may be temporarily suppressed by the presence of liquid within the cavity, and by obstruction of the orifices communicating with bronchial tubes, or of the latter. It may be wanting at one moment, and an act of expectoration may cause it to reappear. Hence, absence of cavity cannot be predicated on the absence of the sign at a single examination. Moreover, if a cavity be not situated near the pulmonary superfices, and solidified lung intervene between it and the walls of the chest, the cavernous sign may be drowned in a loud bronchial respiration. For this reason, while the cavernous sign is positive evidence of a cavity, the absence of the sign is not proof that a cavity does not exist.

In some cases of perforation of lung with pneumothorax, the passage of air to

---

5 Prize Essay on Variations of Pitch in the Sounds obtained by Percussion and Auscultation. Transactions of the American Medical Association, 1852.

and fro through the perforation may give rise to the cavernous respiration. As a rule, however, under these circumstances, another sign is produced, namely, the amphoric respiration.

Broncho-cavernous Respiration.—In this sign, as filename denotes, the characters of the bronchial and the cavernous respiration are combined. These characters may be combined in different ways, as well as in variable proportions. If a cavity be situated in proximity to solidified lung, the quality and pitch of the inspiratory and the expiratory sound may show an admixture of the characters of the two signs and to a practised ear, the combination is distinctly recognizable. This is one of the forms of broncho-cavernous respiration; the sounds are not sufficiently high and tubular for bronchial, nor sufficiently low and blowing for cavernous respiration. Another form consists of an inspiratory sound, the first part of which is tubular, and the latter part cavernous. Examples of this form are not extremely infrequent. Still another form is a cavernous inspiratory, with a bronchial or tubular expiratory sound. In the latter form, the bronchial expiration proceeds from solidified lung situated near the cavity, the intensity of the sound being sufficient to drown the cavernous expiration.

When, as often happens, a cavity is situated in close proximity to, or, it may be, surrounded by solidified lung, the cavernous and the bronchial inspiration are, as it were, in juxtaposition, and such instances offer an excellent opportunity to study the points distinguishing these signs from each other; and, generally, at a short distance the normal vesicular murmur may be found, so that both morbid signs may be compared with the latter. Within a circumscribed area, sometimes, are exemplified the characters of the normal murmur, and of the two morbid signs just mentioned, together with those of the broncho-vesicular respiration.

Amphoric Respiration.—The term amphoric has a significance when applied to auscultatory sounds, analogous to that, which it has in percussion; it denotes a musical intonation which may be compared to the sound produced by blowing upon the open mouth of a decanter or phial. Whenever the respiratory sound has this intonation, it denotes a space containing air which is not expelled with the act of expiration. Air in the pleural cavity, with perforation of lung, is the physical condition most frequently represented by this sign. It is a valuable diagnostic sign in cases of pneumothorax; but it is not always present in that affection, certain accessory conditions being requisite, namely, perforation above the level of liquid, and an unobstructed communication of the bronchial tubes, through the opening, with the pleural space containing air. While, therefore, its presence is significant of pneumothorax, its absence is by no means sufficient to exclude this affection. Not infrequently, it is a sign of a phthisical cavity with rigid walls which do not collapse with the act of expiration. The same contingencies affect its production here as in cases of pneumothorax. Whenever amphoric respiration is present, if pneumothorax be excluded by the absence of the other signs which are diagnostic of this affection, the sign is proof of the existence of a pulmonary cavity, the walls of which are not flaccid. The sign then takes the place of the ordinary cavernous respiration which has been described.

The amphoric sound may accompany either respiration or expiration, or both.

Shortened Inspiration.—The inspiratory sound is somewhat shortened in bronchial or tubular respiration. This modification enters into the characters of that sign, the quality of the sound being tubular, and the pitch high. The shortening is due to the sound ending before the inspiratory act ends; the sound is said to be unfinished. Shortening of the sound occurs, however, when it is not an element in the bronchial respiration. The shortening is then due to the sound not beginning with the inspiratory act; this is distinguished as deferred inspiratory sound. A deferred inspiratory sound not tubular in quality, but more or less vesicular, and not notably raised in pitch, is a sign of pulmonary or vesicular emphysema. It is a sign of diagnostic value in that connection.

The student should note the distinctions just stated which relate to pitch and quality. Suppose an inspiratory sound to be present without an expiratory sound:— if the sound be shortened at the end of the inspiration, the pitch high and the quality tubular, it is bronchial respiration, denoting complete or considerable solidification of lung, but if the shortening be at the beginning of inspiration, the pitch comparatively low, and vesicular quality be appreciable, the sign denotes emphysema, The differential points thus are, the inspiratory sound unfinished or deterred, the pitch high or low, and the quality tubular or vesicular. Attention to these points is essential in order to avoid error in the interpretation of the sign.

Prolonged Expiration.—The length of the expiratory sound in health varies in different persons. The sound is sometimes considerably prolonged; it may be nearly as long as the sound of inspiration. There is no difficulty in recognizing this as a normal peculiarity, from the fact that the murmur has the pitch and quality of health. An unusual length of the expiratory sound, within the range of health, is usually observed at the summit of the chest, and especially on the right side. It is important to bear in mind that at the summit of the chest on the right side, and sometimes also on the left side, a prolonged expiratory sound, more or less raised in pitch, and tubular in quality, may be a normal peculiarity. It follows that a prolonged, and even a high and tubular expiration at the summit of the chest, must not be reckoned as a morbid sign unless it be associated with other signs denoting disease. The laws of the disparity between the two sides of the chest at the summit are to be taken into account (*vide* p. 79).

If the expiration be longer on the left, than on the right side, it is abnormal; so, also, is a high-pitched tabular expiration heard on the left and not on the right side.

The significance of an abnormally prolonged expiration depends on its pitch and quality. If it be high and tubular, it denotes solidification of lung. It is, in fact, bronchial respiration. As already stated, in bronchial or tubular respiration, the inspiratory sound is sometimes wanting, and the presence of the sign is then to be determined by the characters, relating to pitch and quality, of the expiratory sound. The same statement holds true with respect to broncho-vesicular respiration, when this approximates to the bronchial. At the summit of the chest, the characters of the inspiratory sound, and associated morbid signs, always enable the auscultator to determine whether a prolonged high and tubular expiration be, or be not, abnormal. A prolonged expiration, which is low in pitch and blowing in quality, that is, with the characters of health, aside from length, may belong to a cavernous expiration. This is to be determined by the characters of the inspiration, and by other associated signs. Exclusive of cavernous respiration, an abnormally prolonged expiratory sound of low pitch and non-tubular, denotes vesicular emphysema. It is associated then with a weakened and deferred inspiratory sound. A prolonged expiratory sound, in cases of emphysema, is invariably low and non-tubular. If it have not these characters, it is not a sign of emphysema, but belongs to bronchial or broncho-vesicular respiration. Attention to these differential points is to be enjoined upon the student.

A prolonged expiration at the summit of the chest on the right side is sometimes incorrectly considered to be evidence of phthisis. It is to be recollected, in the first place, that prolongation of this sound with a normal pitch and quality, is never evidence of solidification of lung either from phthisis or any other disease; and in the second place, even if the pitch be high, and the quality tubular, that it is not to be regarded as abnormal, provided the inspiratory sound is unchanged, and other signs of disease are not present.

Interrupted Respiration.—To this sign have been applied other names, such as ***jerking, wavy, cogged wheel,*** and by French writers the names entrecoupée *and* saccadée. The modification is either of the inspiration or of the expiration, or of both. The inspiratory, however, much more frequently than the expiratory, sound is interrupted. The sound, instead of being continuous, is broken into one, two, or more parts. This is the characteristic of the sign. If, at the same time, there be alterations in pitch and quality, the interruption is merely incidental to other signs; namely, the bronchial, broncho-vesicular, or cavernous respiration. To constitute it a distinct sign, the interruption must be the only appreciable change. Thus limited, the sign has but little diagnostic value.

Interrupted respiration is sometimes found in healthy persons. It is confined to the summit of the chest, and oftener on the left than the right side. Existing without any other signs, therefore, it is not evidence of disease. It is of value only in the diagnosis of phthisis. Associated with other signs, when the latter are not marked, it is entitled to b certain amount of weight in the diagnosis.

Interrupted respiratory sounds, of course, occur when there is interruption in the respiratory movements. This happens in cases of pleurisy, pleurodynia, or intercostal neuralgia. Owing to the pain caused by the movements in respiration, the patient may breathe, not continuously, but with a series of jerking movements. Sometimes interrupted breathing is observed in persons who are excited or agitated when auscultation is practised. In all these instances, interruption in the respiratory sounds is found over the whole chest, whereas, when it is an abnormal sign in cases of phthisis, it is limited to the summit on one side of the chest, and there is no interruption manifested in the mode of breathing.

Reviewing the foregoing signs, they may be distributed into three classes, as follows: 1st. Signs, the distinctive characters of which relate to either the absence or the intensity of sound, This class an braces (a) increased intensity of tin- vesicular murmur; (b) diminished intensity of the vesicular murmur; and (c) suppression of respiratory sound. 2d. Signs, the distinctive characters of which relate especially to pitch and quality. In this class belong, (a) bronchial or tubular respiration; (b) broncho vesicular respiration; (c) cavernous respiration; (d) broncho-cavernous respiration, and (e) amphoric respiration. 3d. Signs, the distinctive character of which relate especially to rhythm, namely, (a) shortened inspiration; (b) prolonged expiration; and (c) interrupted respiration.

Adventitious Respiratory Sounds, or Rales.

Adventitious respiratory sounds, or, adopting the French term, rales, are distinguished from the morbid signs already considered, by the fact that they have no analogues in health; in other words, they are not normal sounds abnormally modified, but wholly new sounds. A convenient classification of these signs is based on the different anatomical situations in which they are produced. This classification is as follows: 1st. Laryngeal and tracheal rales; 2d. Bronchial rales; 3d. Vesicular rale; 4d. Cavernous rales; 5th. Pleural rales; and 6th. Indeterminate rales. Compared with each other, as regards their characters, they admit of being divided into dry and moist rales, the latter being evidently due to the presence of liquid.

Laryngeal and Tracheal Rales.—The rales produced within the larynx and trachea may be either moist or dry. The moist or bubbling sounds are produced when mucus or other liquid accumulates in these sections of the air tubes. This occurs frequently in the moribund state, and the sounds are then known as the "death rattles." When not incident to this state, they denote either insensibility to the presence of liquid, as in coma, or inability to effect the removal of the liquid by acts of expectoration. The sounds are heard at a distance. They exemplify, on a large scale, moist or bubbling auscultatory sounds which are produced within the bronchial tubes. The dry rales produced within the larynx or trachea are caused by spasm of the glottis, and by diminution of the calibre, either at or below the glottis, from œdema, exudation, the presence of a foreign body, or the pressure of a tumor. The dry sounds are distinguished as whistling, wheezing, crowing, whooping, etc. They are heard at a distance, and they also exemplify auscultatory sounds representing analogous conditions in the bronchial tubes. Characteristic sounds produced at the glottis by spasm enter into the diagnosis of certain affections, namely, laryngismus stridulus, pertussis, croup, and aneurism involving excitation of the recurrent laryngeal nerve. Other sounds are due to paralysis of the laryngeal muscles. Again, dry sounds, called stridor, produced by stenosis of the trachea from the pressure of an aneurismal or other tumor, cicatrization of ulcers, and morbid growths, are of diagnostic importance. Although audible without auscultation, these different sounds, with reference to the precise situation at which they are produced, may sometimes be studied with advantage by means of the stethoscope.

Moist Bronchial Rales

The moist bronchial rales are bubbling sounds produced in different branches of the bronchial tree. They are sounds of which the "tracheal rattles" are an exaggerated type. They may be imitated by blowing into liquids through tubes differing in size. The bubbles seem to be large or small, according to the size of the bronchial tubes in which they are produced. Apparent differences in the size of the bubbles are distinguished by the names coarse and fine. In the primary and secondary bronchial branches the moist sounds are relatively quite coarse; they are less so in tubes of the third or fourth dimensions; in smaller tubes they become fine, and in those of minute size they become quite fine. Extremely fine bubbling sounds constitute what is known as the subcrepitant rale, so called because it approaches in character to the crepitant rale produced within the air vesicles and bronchioles. We may thus judge of the size of the bronchial tubes in which the rales are produced by their comparative coarseness or fineness. Frequently, however, coarse and fine rales are intermingled, and generally those which are either coarse or fine are not uniform, but appear to be of unequal size. In all the varieties of the moist bronchial rales, the bubbling character of the sounds is sufficiently distinctive for their recognition. The differentiation of the subcrepitant from the crepitant rale alone involves some nice points of distinction.

Coarse bubbling rales sometimes occur in acute bronchitis affecting the larger bronchial tubes. Their occurrence is exceptional, because, in general, the mucus within the tubes does not accumulate sufficiently and is too consistent for the production of bubbling sounds. These rales occur in cases in which the mucus is unusually thin and either more abundant than usual or an accumulation takes place in consequence of inability to expectorate freely. These conditions are wanting in the majority of the cases of ordinary acute bronchitis. A muco-purulent liquid in cases of chronic bronchitis is better suited for the production of bubbling sounds than simple mucus. Moreover, coarse rales are heard oftener in children than in adults, because the former do not voluntarily expectorate as freely as the latter. Serous transudation (bronchorrhœa) into tubes of large size may give rise to coarse bubbling rales, and also the presence of blood in some cases of profuse hemorrhage. In bronchitis and bronchorrhœa the rales are heard on both sides of the chest. The bubbling rales, whether coarse or fine, are heard either with the act of inspiration or of expiration, or with both acts.

Fine bubbling sounds and the subcrepitant rale occur in various pathological connections. The characters of the subcrepitant rale are to be borne in mind with reference to the discrimination from the crepitant. The most distinctive character is the moist sound or bubbling; this is sufficiently appreciable. Other characters are the occurrence frequently, but not constantly, in expiration as well as in inspiration, and the inequality of the fine bubbling sounds.

The subcrepitant rale, existing over the chest on both sides, is diagnostic of bronchitis affecting the smaller bronchial tubes (capillary bronchitis), when taken in connection with other signs and the symptoms. The rale exists on both sides, because this, as well as bronchitis affecting the larger tubes, is a bilateral affection. The sign is of great practical value in that pathological connection. The rale also occurs on both sides, and is more or less diffused in pulmonary œdema. This pathological connection is shown by the associated physical signs, together with the symptoms. In so-called capillary bronchitis, the bubbling is due to the presence of thin mucus, and in pulmonary œdema to serous transudation within the small bronchial ramifications.

Fine bubbling or a subcrepitant rale has other pathological connections, as follows:—

1. It occurs in lobar pneumonia during the stage of resolution. Here it is due to the presence of mucus from a bronchitis limited to the affected lobe or lobes, and, in a measure, to liquefied pneumonic exudation. It is considered as denoting commencing and progressing resolution in pneumonia. Sometimes it is intermingled with rales which are more or less coarse.

2. In circumscribed pneumonia, hemorrhagic infarctus, and pulmonary apo-

plexy, the fine or subcrepitant rale, often associated with those which are more or less coarse, denotes the presence of mucus or blood within the bronchial tubes. The rales are localized in a space, or in spaces, corresponding to the situation and extent of the affection.

3. During and shortly after a hemoptysis, fine rales limited to a particular situation are sometimes heard, proceeding from blood in the small bronchial tubes, and indicating the place of the hemorrhage.

4. A purulent liquid admits of bubbling much more readily than mucus; hence, in cases of chronic bronchitis with an expectoration of pus, fine and coarse bronchial rales are more frequent than in acute bronchitis. Pus, also, may be present within bronchial tubes of small size, not as a product of bronchitis, but from the evacuation of an abscess of either the pulmonary parenchyma, of the liver, or some other adjacent part, and from perforation of lung in some cases of empyema.

5. In the different stages of phthisis, moist bronchial rales are usually present. The liquid in the tubes, if the disease be advanced, is derived, in part, from associated bronchitis, and, in part, from liquefied tuberculous exudation. The bubbling sounds may be more or less coarse or fine, and both are often intermingled. Early in the disease before softening of the exudation has taken place, fine bubbling or the subcrepitant rale, limited to the summit of the chest, is an important diagnostic sign. It belongs among the accessory physical signs on which the diagnosis may depend. Here the liquid is derived from a coexisting circumscribed bronchitis.

In cases of fibroid phthisis, or cirrhosis of lung, moist rales, coarse and fine, are generally more or less abundant, and diffused over the whole, or the greater part, of the chest on the affected side.

In the foregoing account of the moist bronchial rales, the subcrepitant rale is not reckoned as a sign distinct from fine babbling sounds. Inasmuch as the mechanism and the significance are the same, and not easy to draw a line of demarcation between the two, the distinction is unimportant. It is sufficient to bear in mind that very fine bubbling sounds are called subcrepitant, because they are somewhat analogous to the crepitant rale. The point which distinguish the latter are, however, well marked, as will appear when the characters of that sign are considered. The moist rales are often called mucous. This name is obviously inappropriate, since, not only are the sounds produced by other liquids than mucus, but other liquids are best suited for their production, especially in the large and medium-sized tubes.

The moist bronchial rales, whether coarse or fine, vary in pitch accordingly as the lung surrounding the tubes in which they are produced is, or is not, solidified. If the lung be solidified, the pitch is high; if there be no solidification, the pitch is comparatively low. Thus, the pitch of the rales is high in the second stage of pneumonia and in phthisis with considerable solidification, whereas the pitch is low in bronchitis and pulmonary œdema. If, therefore, the respiratory sound be suppressed, it is easy to determine by the pitch of these rales whether the lung be solidified or not, and to judge measureably of the degree of solidification. Attention to the pitch in this connection is sometimes of value in diagnosis.

Dry Bronchial Rales.

All adventitious sounds, which are not moist, produced within the air tubes below the trachea, are embraced under the name ***dry bronchial rales.*** The sounds are numerous and varied in character. They are often musical notes. Frequently they are suggestive of certain familiar sounds, such as the chirping of birds, the cry of a young animal, snoring in sleep, cooing of pigeons, humming of the mosquito, the note of the violoncello, etc. etc. They are often heard at a distance, and characterized as wheezing sounds. An interrupted, clicking sound is not uncommon. All these varieties are practically unimportant, and it would be a needless refinement to consider particular varieties as distinct signs. The only distinction which it is desirable to make is into the sibilant and sonorous rales. This distinction is based on difference in pitch; sibilant rales are high, and sonorous rales are low in pitch. As a rule, the sibilant rales are produced in the small and the sonorous rales in the larger sized bronchial tubes. The sounds may accompany either inspiration or expiration, or both. The sibilant and sonorous rales are often intermingled. There may be sibilant rales with inspiration, and sonorous rales with expiration, within the same situation. Moreover, these rales are found often to vary from minute to minute, being at one instant sibilant and at another sonorous. Their recognition involves no difficulty. There are no other adventitious sounds with which they are liable to be confounded.

The physical condition represented by the dry rales is generally a narrowing of the air tubes at certain points, and especially in consequence of spasm of the bronchial muscular fibres. The latter constitutes the essential pathological condition in a paroxysm of asthma; and in this affection the dry rales are always marked. Their diagnostic importance relates chiefly to asthma. Both sibilant and sonorous rales are present and diffused over the entire chest. Wheezing sounds with expiration are heard by the patient, and by others at a distance. A single paroxysm of asthma affords an opportunity for the student to observe all the varieties and fluctuations of these rales. Taken in connection with other signs and the symptoms, the rales are pathognomonic of asthma.

More or less spasm of the bronchial muscular fibres occurs in certain cases of bronchitis, without being sufficiently great and extensive to give rise to a paroxysm of asthma, or own any embarrassment of respiration. Under these circumstances, the rales are less marked and diffused. An asthmatic element may be said to enter, more or less, into these cases. Narrowing of bronchial tubes by tenacious mucus which gives rise to no bubbling sounds, and, perhaps, unequal swelling of the mucous membrane, may also occasion sibilant and sonorous rales.

Dry rales at the summit of the chest are not infrequent in cases of phthisis, due to spasm, the presence of mucus, or to swelling of the mucous membrane. They are sometimes quite annoying to phthisical patients.

Clicking sounds are suggestive of the sudden separation of tenacious mucus from the walls of the bronchial tubes. These are sufficiently common in bronchitis and in phthisis.

Vesicular or Crepitant Rale.

This is the only vesicular rale. It is usually considered to be produced within the air vesicles, but, probably, the terminal bronchial tubes or bronchioles participate in its production.

It is to be distinguished from very fine bubbling sounds, or the subcrepitant rale. The points of distinction are as follows: The sounds are not moist but dry; they are crackling, not bubbling in character. They may be defined to be very fine, dry, crackling sounds. This point of difference is very distinctive. There are, however, other differential points. The crackling sounds are equal, whereas, fine bubbling sounds are unequal, that is, they give the impression of bubbles of unequal size. The crepitating sounds are heard at the end of the inspiratory act, and especially at the end of a forced inspiration, the subcrepitant rale, on the other hand, being heard often with or near the beginning of inspiration, and, perhaps, ceasing before the end of the inspiratory act. Another distinctive feature is the abrupt development of the crepitant rale; a shower of crackles, as it were, springs up at the end of a forced inspiration. Finally, the rale is never heard in expiration. The apparent exceptions to this statement are instances in which the crepitant and the subcrepitant rale are associated. This is not very infrequent, and, with a practical knowledge of the characters of each, it is by no means difficult to appreciate the combination of the two signs. In fact, the combination affords an excellent opportunity to illustrate the distinctive characters of each; the fine bubbling at or near the beginning of inspiration, followed by the fine crackling at the end of this act, and the former reproduced in the act of expiration.

There are various modes in which the crepitant rale may be imitated, for examples, rubbing together a lock of hair near the ear, throwing fine salt upon live coals or into a heated vessel, igniting a train of gunpowder, and alternately pressing and separating the thumb and finger moistened with a solution of gum-arabic and held near the ear. A perfect representation is afforded by squeezing a piece of an artificial preparation known as the India-rubber sponge, and observing the sound produced by the separation of the walls of the interstices when the piece expands from its elasticity. This preparation, which has now gone out of use, exemplified the true mechanism of the sign as described, first, by the late Dr. Carr, of Canandaigua, N. Y., in an article published in the American Journal of Medical Sciences in October, 1842[6].

The crepitant rale is the diagnostic sign of pneumonia. It very rarely occurs in any other pathological connection. Of all respiratory signs, this is most entitled to be called pathognomonic. It belongs especially to the first stage of acute pneumonia. It is not invariably present, but it occurs in the majority of cases of acute pneumonia. In the second stage, or the stage of solidification, the rale generally disappears. It not infrequently is reproduced in the stage of resolution, and it is then called the returning crepitant rale. In the latter stage it is often found in combination with the subcrepitant rale. The practical value of this sign relates chiefly to the diagnosis of

---

6 Vide article by the author in the New York Monthly, Med. Journ. for Feb. 1869.

pneumonia.

It is stated that the crepitant rale is sometimes found in cases of pulmonary œdema, and during or directly after an attack of hemoptysis. If it ever occur in these cases, the instances must be extremely rare. The statement is perhaps based on the occurrence of the subcrepitant, this being confounded with the crepitant rale. It occurs transiently under the following circumstances: a patient who has been confined for Borne time in bed, lying on the back, and much enfeebled with any disease, if suddenly raised to a sitting posture and auscultated, a crepitant rale is often found on the posterior aspect of the chest at the end of a forced inspiration. The rale disappears after a few forced inspirations. It is heard, not on one side only, but on both sides. The explanation is, that during the recumbent posture continued for some time, and the patient breathing feebly, enough of the air vesicles and bronchioles become agglutinated by means of a little sticky transudation to give rise to crackling sounds in a few forced inspirations. It may be of use to mention that if the stethoscope be applied to the anterior surface of a chest much covered with hair, the movements of the pectoral extremity of the instrument in the act of inspiration may produce a sound identical with the crepitant rale.

A crepitant rale at the summit of the chest, within a circumscribed space, is one of the accessory signs of phthisis. It denotes a circumscribed pneumonia which clinical experience shows to be generally secondary to phthisis; hence the diagnostic significance of the sign.

Cavernous or Gurgling Rale.

A pulmonary cavity of considerable size, containing a certain quantity of liquid, and communicating freely with bronchial tubes, furnishes a rale which is characteristic. The character of the sound is expressed as fully as possible by the term gurgling. The sound is produced by large bubbling and the agitation of the liquid within the cavity. It may be compared to the sound produced by the boiling of a liquid in a flask or large test-tube. The sound is sometimes high pitched and amphoric, but generally it is low in pitch. It is heard with more or less intensity within a circumscribed space almost invariably at or near the summit of the chest; but, if intense, the sound is diffused, and it may be sometimes heard at a distance. Its diagnostic importance relates to the advanced stage of phthisis. The rale is heard chiefly or exclusively in the act of inspiration. It may be produced by the act of coughing sometimes with greater intensity than by respiration.

Pleural Rales. Friction Sounds. Metallic Tinkling. Splashing.

The signs embraced under the name pleural rales are, 1st. Sounds produced by the rubbing together of the pleural surfaces, and hence called friction sounds; 2d. Metallic tinkling; and 3d. Splashing or succussion sounds.

Friction Sounds.—Movements of the pleural surfaces upon each other take place in inspiration and expiration; but in health these movements occasion no sound. Sounds are produced when the surfaces are covered with a glutinous matter preventing the normal continuous, unobstructed movements, and when the surfaces are roughened with dense lymph or other morbid products. The sounds are generally interrupted, that is, two, three, or more sounds occur during the act of inspiration or expiration, or during both acts. The intensity of the sounds varies much in different cases. A slight grazing sound only may be heard, or, on the other hand, the sounds may be so loud as to be heard by the patient, and by others at a distance. The character of the sounds is variable. The slight rubbing or grazing character may be imitated by placing over the ear the palmar surface of one hand, and moving over its dorsal surface slowly the pulpy portion of a finger of the other hand. In some instances, however, the rough character of the sounds is expressed by such terms as rasping, grating, and creaking. In these instances the sounds denote density of the morbid product which roughens the pleural surfaces. In connection with very rough friction sounds, vibration of the walls of the chest or fremitus is sometimes perceived by palpation.

Aside from the character of the sounds as just stated, they are distinguised by their apparent nearness to the ear; they seem sometimes to be produced upon the surface of the chest. They are sometimes intensified by firm pressure of the stethoscope upon the chest. After a little practical knowledge of these sounds, they can hardly be confounded with any other rales.

Pleuritic friction sounds generally denote pleurisy. In cases of pleurisy with effusion, slight rubbing or grazing is sometimes heard before much liquid accumulates within the pleuritic cavity. The physical conditions, however, after the effusion has been removed, are much more favorable for the production of friction sounds, and they are often now rough in character. They may be transient, or they may continue for a considerable period, their duration depending on the arrest of the movements of the pleural surfaces by means of either agglutination with lymph, or adhesion from the growth of areolar tissue.

Pleuritic friction sounds occur not infrequently in cases of pneumonia, denoting, in this connection, coexisting pleurisy.

Slight rubbing or grazing at the summit of the chest is one of the accessory signs of phthisis. It denotes a circumscribed, dry pleurisy which, as clinical experience shows, is generally secondary to phthisis, and, hence, the diagnostic significance of the sign.

In the foregoing instances in which friction sounds are stated to occur, their significance relates to pleurisy. In some rare instances the sounds are produced by miliary tubercles or carcinomatous tumors projecting beyond die plane of the visceral pleural surface, without pleuritic inflammation.

Metallic Tinkling.—This is a vocal as well as a respiratory sign. It is also produced by acts of coughing, and sometimes by the act of deglutition. The name expresses the distinctive character of the sign. It consists in a series of tinkling sounds of a high pitched, silvery or metallic tone. The number of sounds varies from a single sound, to two, three, or more sounds, during an act of either inspiration or expiration. It occurs irregularly, that is, it is not present in every act of breathing, but is heard at variable intervals. It may sometimes be produced by forced, when it is not beard in tranquil, breathing. The sounds can only be confounded with tinkling sounds sometimes produced within the stomach. The latter, however, are easily discriminated by their situation, and the absence of associated signs denoting the affections of the chest in which the sign occurs.

Metallic tinkling is the sign of pneumothorax with perforation of lung. In the great majority of the cases in which it is found, it is diagnostic of this affection. It is, however, always associated with other physical signs corroborative of the diagnosis.

It is a rare sign, in cases of phthisis, of a large cavity, the conditions for its production being analogous to those in pneumo hydrothorax, namely, a space of considerable size containing air and liquid, the space communicating with bronchial tubes.

***Splashing; or, Succussion Sounds.*—**This sign is produced by succussion, which is reckoned as one of the different methods of physical exploration. Sounds thus produced are not infrequently heard at some distance; generally, however, succussion is practised while the ear is applied to the chest, so that, properly enough, the sign may be embraced among the auscultatory signs, although not produced by respiration.

Splashing is pathognomonic of one affection, namely, pneumo-hydrothorax. It is especially valuable as a sign of that affection because it is almost invariably available. The instances are extremely few in which the sign is wanting when air and liquid are contained in the pleural cavity. It is obtained by jerking the body of the patient raised. These characters are in contrast with the diffusion, distance, and lowness of pitch of the normal vocal resonance. The intensity of the sound is variable; it may be greater or less than the intensity of the normal resonance. A concentrated, high-pitched sound, however feeble, is not less a sign of complete or considerable solidification of lung, that is, it is not less bronchophony, than when the sound is intense.

Vocal fremitus is always to be discriminated from vocal resonance. The fremitus associated with bronchophony may, or may not, be greater than the fremitus of health. Not infrequently the fremitus is less than in health.

It is to be borne in mind that in some healthy persons bronchophony exists al the summit of the chest, especially on the right side, over the primary bronchus. Existing alone in this situation, it may not be abnormal.

Representing complete or considerable solidification of lung, this sign occurs in the different affections in which bronchial or tubular respiration has been seen to occur (***vide*** page 98), namely, lobar pneumonia, phthisis, chronic or fibroid pneumonia, condensation of lung from either pleuritic effusion, the accumulation of air in the pleural cavity or the pressure of a tumor, collapse of pulmonary lobules, coagulation of blood within the air vesicles, and carcinoma of lung.

For the production of bronchophony, a less degree of solidification is requisite than for the production of bronchial or tubular respiration. Hence, bronchophony may be associated with a broncho-vesicular, as well as with a purely bronchial, respiration. This is illustrated in the resolving stage of pneumonia. When resolution has progressed sufficiently for the bronchial to give place to the broncho-vesicular respiration, well-marked bronchophony is often found to continue, ceasing at a later period in the resolving stage.

The apparent nearness to the ear of the vocal sound in bronchophony is wanting if a certain quantity of liquid intervene between the solidified lung and the walls of the chest at the situation auscultated. The voice under these conditions seems to be more or less distant. This difference is readily appreciated. With this apparent distance of the bronchophonic voice, in some instances is associated the modification which is characteristic of another sign, namely, ægophony.

Whispering Bronchophony.

The characters of this sign correspond to those of the expiratory sound in the bronchial or tubular respiration (*vide* p. 98). The sound is more or less intensified, high in pitch, and tubular in quality. If the patient pronounce numerals in a forced whisper, the characters are generally more marked than in the expiratory sound in forced breathing. The significance of this sign is the same as that of the bronchial or tubular respiration, and of bronchophony with the loud voice.

Ægophony.

This sign is a modification of bronchophony. As regards concentration and pitch, it has the characters of bronchophony, the distinctive features being apparent distance from the ear, and a tremulousness or a bleating tone. From the latter the name is derived, the term signifying the cry of the goat. The features which distinguish the sign from bronchophony are readily enough appreciated, and it represents a physical condition added to solidification of lung. This physical condition is the presence of liquid effusion. The sign is rarely present in cases of large effusion. It occurs usually when the chest is about half filled with liquid, and the lung at the level of the liquid is sufficiently condensed to give rise to bronchophony. This condition, under these circumstances, involves agglutination of lung above the portion condensed by pressure. The sign also sometimes occurs in cases of pleuro-pneumonia, the solidification in these cases being due to pneumonic exudation. As a sign of liquid effusion it possesses diagnostic value, although, owing to the fact that the existence of effusion is easily determined by other signs, it may be said to be superfluous.

Increased Vocal Resonance and Fremitus.

The distinctive character of this sign is an increase of the intensity of the resonance without notable change in other respects. The resonance may be more or less intensified, but it is distant, diffused, and comparatively low in pitch; in other words, the characters of bronchophony are wanting. The differential points between bronchophony and increased resonance should be clearly apprehended, bearing in mind that the intensity of the sound in bronchophony may, or may not, be greater than the normal resonance.

Increased vocal resonance occurs when the lung is solidified, the solidification not sufficient in degree to produce bronchophony. Lung slightly or moderately solidified gives rise to an increase of intensity; if the solidification become considerable or complete, bronchophony takes the place of the simple increase of intensity. Thus, at an early period in pneumonia, increased vocal resonance precedes bronchophony; and in the stage of resolution the reverse of this takes place, namely, increased vocal resonance follows bronchophony, the latter ceasing when resolution has progressed to a certain extent.

Contrary to what would perhaps be anticipated, in the instances just cited, the intensity of the sound when bronchophony is present may be not only not increased, but diminished below that of health; that is, in the first stage of pneumonia, the increased intensity may cease when bronchophony occurs, and return when bronchophony disappears.

Increase of the vocal resonance occurs in connection with pulmonary cavities. Over a cavity of considerable size situated near the superficies of the lung, the vocal resonance is sometimes extremely intense without any bronchophonic characters. The latter, if present, denote considerable solidification either around the cavity, or between it and the walls of the chest. From the presence or the absence of bronchophonic characters with greatly increased intensity of resonance, the auscultator can judge whether the cavity be, or be not, in proximity to considerable solidification of lung.

Irrespective of the cavernous stage of phthisis, the sign is of diagnostic importance in the different affections which involve moderate or slight solidification of lung, namely, pneumonia early in the disease and in the stage of resolution, phthisis, over the compressed lung in pleurisy with moderate effusion, collapse of pulmonary lobules, hemorrhagic infarctus, and carcinoma of lung. Into the diagnosis of all these affections, both bronchophony and increased vocal resonance enter; the former, when solidification is considerable or complete, and the latter when it is slight or moderate. Increased vocal resonance is especially valuable in the diagnosis of early or incipient phthisis. An abnormal resonance, however slight, at the summit of the chest on one side, is an important sign in that affection. In determining an abnormal resonance on the right side, either at the summit or elsewhere, allowance must always be made for the normally greater resonance on this side.

Increased vocal resonance has the same import as the broncho-vesicular respiration. These two signs, however, are not always in the same proportion; that is, the characters of the latter may be marked out of proportion to the amount of the increase of the vocal resonance, and *vice versa.*

Increased vocal fremitus generally accompanies increased vocal resonance, and it denotes solidification of lung. Fremitus, however, and resonance are not always in equal proportion, that is, either may be increased more than the other. An increased fremitus is sometimes of value in the diagnosis of phthisis. The greater fremitus on the right side of the chest is always to be borne in mind, and due allowance is to be made for this disparity in determining that the fremitus is increased.

Increased Bronchial Whisper.

The significance of this sign is the same as that of increased vocal resonance and the broncho-vesicular respiration; it represents the same physical condition as the two latter signs, namely, solidification of lung, greater or less, but below the degree requisite to give rise to bronchophony and bronchial respiration. Its diagnostic application is, therefore, involved in the same pulmonary affections.

The characters of the sign are those which belong to the expiratory sound in the broncho-vesicular respiration. They consist, therefore, of increase of intensity and length, a quality more or less tubular, and the pitch raised, these modifications of the normal expiratory sound varying in degree between the slightest appreciable morbid change and a close approximation to the bronchophonic whisper. The modifications in degree correspond to the degree of solidification. To appreciate the characters of this sign, it must be studied in comparison with those of the normal bronchial whisper in different portions of the chest. The most important of the diagnostic applications of the sign is in cases of phthisis in its early stage. In this application, the points of normal disparity between the two sides of the chest at the summit are to be borne in mind, and due allowance made for them (*vide* page 88).

A greater intensity of the bronchial whisper at the right summit is not evidence of disease; but greater intensity at the left summit is always abnormal. As a rule, the pitch of the normal bronchial whisper at the left, is higher than that at the right summit; if, therefore, with a greater intensity of the whisper at the right summit, it be a matter of doubt whether it denote disease or not, when the pitch is higher at this summit, it is to be considered as morbid.

Cavernous Whisper.—The characters distinctive of the cavernous whisper are those of the expiratory sound in the cavernous respiration, namely, lowness of pitch, and the quality blowing, that is, non-tubular. The intensity and the duration of the sound are variable. It is limited to a circumscribed space corresponding to the situation and size of the cavity. Not infrequently the characters of the sign are brought into contrast with those of whispering bronchophony, or increased bronchial whisper, these latter signs existing in close proximity, and representing solidification of lung in the immediate neighborhood of the cavity. The diagnostic application of this sign is chiefly to advanced phthisis.

Pectoriloquy.—In pectoriloquy, not merely the voice, but the speech, is transmitted through the chest; the auscultator recognizes words uttered by the patient. The student, however, must not expect to be able to carry on a conversation with the patient, by means of the stethoscope. Often single words only can be recognized. To make sure that these are transmitted through the chest, care must be taken to exclude their direct transmission from the patient's mouth, and the auscultator should not know beforehand the words which are to be spoken. If these rules be not observed, the auscultator may err in supposing that the words are transmitted through the chest. When auscultation is practised with one ear, the other should be closed.

The speech with either the loud or the whispered voice may be transmitted, the latter, distinguished as whispering pectoriloquy, being much more frequent than the former; moreover, in determining whispering pectoriloquy, there is less liability to error in mistaking the perception of words coming directly from the mouth for the transmission through the chest. In the production of this sign, much depends on the distinctness with which words are articulated by the patient.

Pectoriloquy belongs among the cavernous signs; but it is by no means exclusively the sign of a cavity; the speech may also be transmitted by solidified lung. It is easy to determine in any case whether the sign denotes a cavity or solidified lung. If, with transmitted speech, the voice have the characters of bronchophony, the sign represents solidification of lung; if, on the other hand, the characters of bronchophony be wanting, the sign represents a cavity. These statements apply equally to the loud and to the whispered voice. Of course, associated signs will be likely to show whether a cavity exists or not. It is to be added that a cavity and solidification of lung existing together, may conjointly be concerned in the production of the sign.

Amphoric Voice or Echo.—This sign is identical in character with amphoric respiration, with which it is usually associated (*vide* page 106). The amphoric intonation may accompany the loud voice and the whisper; generally, it is more appreciable or marked with the latter. Its significance is the same as that of amphoric respiration. As a rule, it represents the conditions in pneumothorax, namely, a large space filled with air and perforation of lung. In this affection it is associated with other signs which suffice for a prompt and positive diagnosis. It is not invariably found in pneumothorax, and it may be present in a case at one time and wanting at another time, its production being dependent on the perforation being above the level of liquid, if the latter exist, and on the bronchial tubes leading to the perforation being unobstructed. When not associated with other signs which are diagnostic of pneumothorax, or pneumo-hydrothorax, it denotes a phthisical cavity of considerable size. It is not infrequently a sign of a phthisical cavity with rigid walls and communicating freely with bronchial tubes. It has this significance whenever pneumothorax can be excluded; and the associated signs in the latter affection are such that its exclusion is always practicable.

The amphoric sound sometimes is observed to follow the oral voice; hence, the name amphoric echo.

Diminished and Suppressed Vocal Resonance.—Diminution and suppression of the normal vocal resonance occur especially when the pleural cavity contains either liquid or air. Whenever the lungs are not in contact with the walls of the chest, the vocal resonance, as a rule, is either notably lessened or wanting. The sign is, therefore, of value in diagnosis in cases of pleurisy with effusion, empyema, hydrothorax, and pneumothorax. When the pleural cavity is partially filled with liquid, there is diminution or suppression of the resonance from the level of the liquid downward; and, generally, just above the level of the liquid, the resonance is increased, owing to condensation of the lung. The sign is well illustrated by the contrast in such cases above and below the level of the liquid. The changes of the level of the liquid with changes in position of the body, may be as well demonstrated by means of vocal resonance as by percussion.

The practical importance of diminished and suppressed vocal resonance relates chiefly to the diagnosis of the affections just named. In this application, however, the associated signs must be taken into account. The vocal resonance may be diminished or suppressed when the lung is completely solidified in the second stage of pneumonia; also in pulmonary œdema, and over the site of an intra-thoracic tumor.

If the vocal resonance be normal, that is, neither increased nor diminished, we are warranted in excluding all the affections which have been named. If this statement is to be qualified in any measure, the exceptional instances are so rare that, practically, they may be disregarded.

Diminished vocal resonance may be found over a pulmonary abscess before the pus is evacuated, and over a cavity filled with liquid. The sign is then limited to a circumscribed space. Obstruction of a bronchial tube diminishes resonance in so far as the column of air is a medium for the conduction of vocal sound.

The normal disparity between the two sides of the chest is to be borne in mind with reference to diminished or suppressed, as well as to increased vocal resonance; otherwise, the relative feebleness of the resonance on the left side in health might be considered to be morbid. The normally greater resonance on the right side renders it easier to determine a morbid diminution on this than on the left side.

Diminished and Suppressed Vocal Fremitus.—This tactile sensation, which is appreciable in auscultation, as a rule, is, on the one hand, increased, and, on the other hand, diminished or suppressed, under the same physical conditions which occasion corresponding modifications of the vocal resonance. Diminished or suppressed vocal fremitus, therefore, has the same diagnostic significance as diminished or suppressed vocal resonance. Usually the abnormal modifications of resonance and fremitus go together, but either may be out of proportion to the other. The signs relating to fremitus thus corroborate those relating to resonance. The former may be marked when the latter admit of doubt. Diminished or suppressed fremitus is valuable in the diagnosis of pleurisy with effusion, empyema, hydrothorax, and pneumothorax.

With regard to vocal fremitus, as to vocal resonance, it is essential to take cognizance of the normal disparity between the two sides of the chest; the greater relative fremitus, on the right side, as a rule, being no less marked than the relatively greater resonance on that side.

Metallic Tinkling.—This sign has the same characters when it accompanies either the loud or whispered voice, or when it is heard with respiration, and, of course, it has the same significance. It may be more marked with acts of speaking than with the respiratory acts.

Signs obtained by Acts of Coughing or Tussive Signs.

Acts of coughing may be made subservient to auscultation of respiratory sounds in two ways: **First,** by the removal of temporary obstruction from the accumulation of mucus within bronchial tubes. If the respiratory murmur be diminished or suppressed over a portion or the whole of one side of the chest, sometimes an act of coughing effects dislodgment of a mass of mucus from either a primary bronchus or one of its subdivisions, and the normal murmur is at once restored. The dependence of the morbid sign upon a temporary obstruction is thus demonstrated. **Second,** by an act of coughing more air is expelled than by an ordinary expiration, and in the following inspiration the vesicles have a wider range of expansion, giving rise to a proportionately loud inspiratory sound; hence, the characters of this sound are more pronounced and can be better studied. For these two objects it is often advisable to request the patient to cough with a certain degree of force.

Acts of coughing, moreover, give rise to auscultatory signs which have their analogues in signs obtained by respiration and the voice. These tussive signs are of less value than the respiratory and vocal signs, and in most cases, owing to the latter being sufficient for diagnosis, they may be said to be superfluous; nevertheless, they may be observed sometimes with advantage. When the conditions are present which are represented by bronchial respiration, bronchophony and the bronchophonic whisper, sounds are obtained which correspond to these in their characters.

of coughing a concussion or shock which is sometimes so forcible as to be painful. This corresponds to an intense vocal resonance. Limited to a circumscribed space, it is a highly significant cavernous sign. A low pitched blowing sound corresponds to the expiratory sound in the cavernous respiration and the cavernous whisper. An amphoric intonation may be heard with acts of coughing, which corresponds to amphoric respiration and amphoric voice. This sign is sometimes more marked with cough than with the breathing and voice. Cavernous gurgling may also be obtained more distinctly with cough than with respiration. Finally, metallic tinkling not infrequently accompanies acts of coughing.

CHAPTER VI.
THE PHYSICAL DIAGNOSIS OF DISEASES OF THE RESPIRATORY SYSTEM.

Affections of the larynx and trachea—Bronchitis seated in large bronchial tubes—Bronchitis seated in small bronchial tubes, or capillary bronchitis—Collapse of pulmonary lobules—Lobular pneumonia—Asthma—Pulmonary or vesicular emphysema—Pleurisy, acute and chronic—Empyema—Hydrothorax—Pneumothorax—Pneumo-hydrothorax—Acute lobar pneumonia—Circumscribed pneumonia—Embolic pneumonia—Hemorrhagic infarctus—Pulmonary apoplexy—Pulmonary gangrene—Pulmonary œdema—Carcinoma of lung—Tumor within the chest—Acute miliary tuberculosis—Phthisis—Fibroid phthisis—Interstitial pneumonia or cirrhosis of lung—Diaphragmatic hernia.

IN the preceding chapters the physical conditions incident to the morbid changes occurring in the affections of the respiratory system have been enumerated; and the physical signs obtained by percussion and auscultation representing these conditions have been considered, severally, as regards their distinctive characters and their significance. The object of this chapter is to group the physical conditions embraced in the different affections of the respiratory system respectively, together with the representative signs on which rests the physical diagnosis of each of the affections. The scope of this manual is limited to the physical diagnosis of these affections; but the fact is not to be lost sight of that in practical medicine physical signs are not to be disassociated from symptoms and pathological laws. An exclusive reliance on physical signs would lead to errors in diagnosis, although, doubtless, errors more important and more frequent necessarily occur when the practitioner ignores percussion and auscultation. The signs furnished by percussion and auscultation only have been thus far considered; but in grouping these in this chapter, signs obtained by other methods of physical exploration will be embraced in so far as they enter into the diagnosis of the different affections of the respiratory system. These different affections will be taken up separately with the exception of those seated in the larynx and trachea. With reference to physical signs the laryngeal and tracheal affections may be considered collectively.

Affections of the Larynx and Trachea.

The physical signs referable to the chest in affections of the larynx and trachea, denote more or less obstruction to the free passage of air through these sections of the air tubes. The obstruction in the different affections involves different pathological conditions. Spasm of the glottis is one of these conditions, constituting the affections known as laryngismus stridulus and spasmodic croup, occurring also as a pathological element in laryngitis, and sometimes in connection with aneurism, or a tumor of some kind, involving the recurrent laryngeal nerve. Another pathological condition is the opposite of this, namely, paralysis of the expanding muscles of the glottis, the vocal chords remaining flaccid, and approximating during inspiration. Other pathological conditions are, œdema of the glottis, swelling of the membrane at the glottis in laryngitis, and, in the adult, submucous infiltration, diphtheritic exudation, cicatrization of ulcers, morbid growths, and the presence of foreign bodies.

In the affections involving the foregoing pathological conditions, percussion and auscultation are of use, *first,* by enabling the physician to exclude all affections within the chest. The absence of signs showing the existence of pulmonary diseases renders it certain that the symptoms denoting embarrassment of respiration are referable to the larynx or trachea. ***Second,*** by means of auscultation the amount of obstruction may be determined more accurately than by the subjective symptoms. The amount of obstruction is represented by a proportionate weakening of the vesicular murmur. This is more reliable as regards determining a dangerous amount of obstruction than the sense of the want of air or the suffering of the patient. The degree of diminution of the vesicular murmur is determinable with the more accuracy the better the auscultator is acquainted with the normal intensity, that is, the intensity prior to the occurrence of obstruction. With this knowledge, the weakening of the murmur is a correct criterion of the amount of obstruction. In all the pathological conditions named, the respiratory murmur is more or less diminished in Intensity on both sides of the chest; there are no signs obtained by percussion, nor do vocal resonance or fremitus offer anything distinctive.

In cases of considerable or great obstruction, inspection furnishes marked signs. The expansion of the chest on both sides is restricted, the lower part of the chest is contracted in the act of inspiration, and in this act the soft parts above the clavicles are depressed. The contrast between these abnormal movements and the normal thoracic movements of the patient is striking and distinctive.

An important application of auscultation is the localization of a foreign body which has been inhaled. If the vesicular murmur on both sides be more or less weakened, the foreign body must be situated in either the larynx or the trachea. If, on the other hand, the vesicular murmur be weakened or suppressed on one side, and increased on the other side; the body is lodged in a primary bronchus. The importance of this application of auscultation before opening the trachea to remove a foreign body, is sufficiently obvious. The situation of a foreign body may be changed from one bronchus to the other by an act of coughing, even after an operation has been commenced; this is, of course, at once determinable by auscultation.

Bronchitis Seated in Large Bronchial Tubes.

In bronchitis, either acute or chronic, as it is ordinarily presented in practice, the inflammation is seated in the large bronchial tubes, in many cases probably not extending beyond the primary bronchi. The physical conditions are, more or less swelling of the mucous membrane, this, however, not being sufficient to occasion any notable obstruction to the free passage of air, and the presence, in different cases, in greater or less quantity, of mucus, muco-purulent matter, pure pus, and serum.

The physical diagnosis involves negative rather than positive points; in other words, the affections from which bronchitis is to be differentiated are excluded by the absence of their diagnostic signs. These affections are pneumonia, pleurisy, and phthisis. Each of these is characterized by the presence of signs, the absence of which warrants its exclusion. In bronchitis there is no disparity between the two sides of the chest in the resonance obtained by percussion, nor in vocal resonance, the bronchial whisper, and fremitus. The swelling of the bronchial mucous membrane may cause some diminution of the intensity of the vesicular murmur, but as the affection is bilateral, and the bronchial tubes on each side are affected equally, both in degree and extent, no appreciable disparity in this respect between the two sides is caused by this physical condition. Weakening or suppression of the murmur over an area greater or less, may be caused by bronchial obstruction from a plug of mucus. This obstruction is sometimes removed by an act of expectoration, after which the murmur is found to have returned, or to have regained its normal intensity.

The foregoing points, taken in connection with the history and symptoms, suffice for the diagnosis. Signs due directly to the disease represent diminished calibre of the tubes at certain points from swelling of the membrane, adhesive mucus, and spasm of bronchial muscular fibres. These signs are the dry bronchial rales. They are rarely prominent, and are oftener absent than present, if the bronchitis be unaccompanied by asthma; hence, they are of little value in the diagnosis. Other signs are the bubbling sounds or the moist bronchial rales. In acute bronchitis, these are oftener absent than present. They occur when there is an unusual quantity of liquid morbid products, or their removal is with difficulty effected by expectoration in consequence of muscular debility or other causes. These rales are abundant and loud in proportion as the liquid within the tubes is either muco-purulent, purulent, or serous in character. They are more or less coarse in proportion to the size of the tubes in which the bubbling takes place.

The diagnostic points, negative and positive, which have been stated, are alike applicable to acute and chronic bronchitis, it being, of course, understood that the affection is primary, that is, not secondary to some other pulmonary disease.

Bronchitis Seated in Small Bronchial Tubes. Capillary Bronchitis. Collapse of Pulmonary Lobules. Lobular Pneumonia.

Inflammation extending into the small tubes (capillary bronchitis) occasions in these the same physical conditions which are incident to bronchitis affecting tubes of large size, namely, swelling of the membrane, and the presence of liquid morbid products. The latter are not as easily removed by expectoration as when they are within large tubes, and, therefore, they are constantly present in greater or less quantity. These conditions in small tubes involve obstruction to the free passage of air to and from the air vesicles; hence, the vast difference as regards the symptoms, the suffering, and the danger. The affection is bilateral, a fact greatly enhancing the gravity of the affection. An incidental physical condition is solidification, generally in disseminated portions of lung, the latter varying in number and size. These portions of solidified lung denote either collapse of pulmonary lobules or lobular pneumonia, or both in conjunction. To this incidental affection, German writers apply the name "Catarrhal pneumonia." Of course, any discussion of pathological questions suggested by these names would be here out of place. With reference to diagnosis it is to be borne in mind that the solidified portions of lung in cases of bronchitis seated in small tubes are especially situated in the lower lobes. Another incidental physical condition is temporary dilatation of the air cells, or vesicular emphysema, seated in the upper lobes. Both of these incidental conditions are bilateral, like the bronchitis with which they are connected. Collapse of pulmonary lobules, or lobular pneumonia, or both, and emphysema occur in only a certain proportion of the cases of bronchitis sealed in small tubes. The signs, therefore, admit of a division into those which relate, 1st, to the bronchitis, and, 2d, to these incidental affections. With reference to the diagnosis, the fact is to be borne in mind that bronchitis seated in small tubes occurs chiefly in children and the aged.

The physical diagnosis of bronchitis seated in small tubes, rests on negative points, together with a positive sign which is uniformly present. This sign is the fine moist bronchial or subcrepitant rale, present on both sides and diffused over the chest. The bubbling sounds are to be distinguished from the fine dry crackling sounds or the crepitant rale, to the characters of which the former in some measure approximate.

The bronchitis gives rise neither to dulness on percussion, nor to any notable change in vocal resonance, or fremitus. The respiratory murmur, if not obscured by rales, is weakened on both sides. Irrespective of being drowned by rales, it may be suppressed by the amount of bronchial obstruction. These are the negative points in the diagnosis. In pulmonary œdema, fine moist bronchial rales are present on both sides, but in this affection there is notable dulness on percussion, and the affection occurs in certain pathological connections, namely, with mitral stenosis, and disease of the kidneys. Acute tuberculosis may present the moist bronchial rales with the negative points, which, in connection with symptoms, characterize bronchitis seated in the small tubes. The differentiation is to be based on differences pertaining to the history and duration, together with the age of the patient.

The coexistence of the incidental affections, namely, collapse of pulmonary lobules, or lobular pneumonia and emphysema, occasions additional signs. If the solidified portions of lung be numerous, or considerable in size, there will be dulness on percussion in circumscribed situations on the posterior aspect of the chest. This will be found on both sides, but perhaps more marked on one side. Broncho-vesicular or the bronchial respiration may be present, together with the vocal signs of solidification, namely, either increased vocal resonance, or bronchophony, and increased vocal fremitus. The pitch of the moist rales produced within solidified portions of lung will be high in pitch, whereas, if solidification do not exist, these rales are comparatively low in pitch. The existence of solidification at any point may be determined by the pitch of the rales, as well as by the foregoing respiratory and vocal signs.

On the anterior aspect of the chest in the upper and middle regions, on both sides, the resonance on percussion is vesiculo-tympanitic, the respiratory murmur weakened or suppressed, and the rhythm altered—in short, the combination of signs which will be stated under the head of emphysema.

In the cases in which the bronchitis occasions great obstruction in the small tubes, and, still more, if collapse of lobules, or lobular pneumonia and emphysema occur, important signs are obtained by inspection. The anterior portion of the chest remains expanded, and retraction of the lower part of the chest takes place in the acts of inspiration.

Asthma.

The pathologico-physical condition in a paroxysm of asthma, is obstruction in the small bronchial tubes attributable to spasm of the bronchial muscular fibres. With this condition is associated a temporary vesicular emphysema, which exists often as a persistent affection in persons who are subject to asthma. If the emphysematous condition already exist, it is increased during the paroxysm of asthma. Bronchitis generally coexists either as a transient or a chronic affection. In an asthmatic paroxysm, therefore, there are present the signs which are proper to asthma, together with those of emphysema, and associated bronchitis may also occasion additional signs.

The physical diagnosis of asthma, like that of bronchitis seated in small tubes, is based on negative points taken in connection with a sign which is invariably present, namely, dry bronchial rales. These rales are more or less intense, and they are diffused over the entire chest. They are generally heard at a distance. The sibilant and sonorous varieties are mingled, and they are constantly changing as regards the character of the sounds.

The negative points are the same as in capillary bronchitis, namely, absence of dulness on percussion, vocal resonance and fremitus also being unaltered. Asthma and bronchitis seated in small tubes agree in the fact that obstruction is the important physical condition. Pathologically they differ essentially in the obstruction being due in the latter affection to bronchial inflammation, and in the former to spasm. The two affections differ in the signs representing these different conditions, fine moist bronchial rales existing in one, and loud diffused dry bronchial rales existing in the other.

Taking the difference as regards the positive physical signs in connection with the history and symptoms, the differentiation of the two affections may be made without difficulty.

The signs which relate to the associated emphysematous condition, are those which are diagnostic of this condition, existing irrespective of asthma; and the physical diagnosis of emphysema will be next considered. Coexisting bronchitis may give rise to moist bronchial rales more or less coarse. These are, however, often wanting, and they are rarely marked during paroxysms of asthma. When present in this pathological connection, they are low in pitch, denoting the absence of solidification of lung.

Pulmonary or Vesicular Emphysema.

This affection, as a rule, is seated exclusively or chiefly in the upper lobes. When it is lobar, in contradistinction from lobular emphysema (in the latter variety the condition existing in comparatively a few disseminated or isolated portions of lung), increase in volume of the affected lobes is an important physical condition standing in relation to certain signs. Diminished range of expansion with acts of inspiration is another physical condition; the affected lobes are in a permanent state of expansion approximating to that at the end of the inspiratory act. It follows from these conditions that the amount of air is in excess of the normal proportion to the solids and liquids in the affected lobes. Both lungs are affected, that is, the affection is bilateral. In the great majority of cases chronic bronchitis coexists, and patients affected with emphysema are often, but by no means invariably, subject to paroxysms of asthma. Not infrequently an asthmatic element, with or without pronounced paroxysms of asthma, exists much of the time in connection with emphysema. The emphysematous condition, as a rule, with few exceptions, is greater in the upper lobe of the left than of the right lung. A rare condition, which is generally included under the name emphysema, differs materially from the ordinary form of this affection. This condition is that also known as senile atrophy of the lungs. The volume of the lungs is not increased in this variety of emphysema, the proportion of air over the solids is, however, in excess, owing to the diminution of the latter from atrophy.

The diagnostic evidence obtained by percussion is quite distinctive of ordinary lobar emphysema. The resonance over the upper and middle regions of the chest on both sides is vesiculo-tympanitic, that is, the intensity of the resonance is abnormally increased, the quality is a combination of the vesicular and tympanitic, and the pitch is more or less raised. Owing to the fact that the emphysema is greater on the left than on the right side, the vesiculo-tympanitic resonance is more marked on the left side. The difference in intensity between the two sides may lead to the error of regarding the resonance on the right side as dulness. The error is avoided by attention to the pitch and the quality of the resonance. If dulness existed on the right side, the pitch of the sound should be higher on that side; on the other hand, if the difference in intensity be due to the greater amount of emphysema on the left side, the pitch is higher on that side, and the quality vesiculo-tympanitic. The attention of the student is particularly called to the foregoing points of distinction. Assuming that a vesiculo-tympanitic resonance exists anteriorly on both sides, and that it is marked on the left as contrasted with the right side, how is the existence of this sign on the right side to be determined? The answer is, the resonance over the upper is to be compared with that over the lower lobe of the right lung. Percussing first over the upper lobe of the right lung, and second over the lower lobe of this lung, that is, posteriorly, below the scapula, or in the infra-axillary region, the vesiculo-tympanitic resonance over the upper lobe is rendered manifest. In a series of patients affected with emphysema, the uniformity of the results of percussion is very striking; anteriorly, over the left side, the resonance is vesiculo-tympanitic as compared with the resonance on the right side, and the resonance is shown to be vesiculo-tympanitic on the right side anteriorly as compared with the resonance posteriorly below the scapula.

As regards the abnormal modifications of the respiratory murmur in emphysema, there is, first, weakened or, it may be, suppressed respiratory sounds without notable change in pitch or quality. Diminished intensity of the murmur exists over the upper lobes on both sides, as compared with the murmur over the lower lobes; and in most cases the greater diminution or the suppression is on the left rather than on the right side. Exceptions to the latter statement may be caused by obstruction of the bronchial tubes on the right and not on the left side by an accumulation of mucus, and, in rare instances, by the fact that the emphysema is greater on the right side. ***Second,*** modifications in rhythm are not infrequent. These consist in a shortened (deferred) inspiratory, and a prolonged expiratory sound. In some instances an inspiratory sound is wanting, and an expiratory sound is alone heard. The prolonged expiratory sound in emphysema is always low in pitch and blowing or non-tubular in quality, in these respects differing from the prolonged expiration which denotes solidification of lung, the latter being high in pitch and tubular in quality. These essential points of difference I claim to have been the first to point out distinctly.

The foregoing signs obtained by percussion and auscultation are those which are in a positive sense diagnostic of emphysema. Associated with these are certain important negative points, as follows: vocal resonance, vocal fremitus, and bronchial whisper are not notably altered. These negative points suffice to exclude other affections than emphysema.

Signs obtained by inspection are quite distinctive of this affection. Emphysema, existing in a marked degree, causes a characteristic deformity of the chest; the anterior surface is bulging, giving to the chest an abnormally rounded, bow-windowed, or barrel-shaped appearance, the lower part appearing to be contracted. This deformity occurs when the emphysema has been developed in early life. The movements of the chest in inspiration are characteristic. In tranquil breathing there is but little movement of the upper and middle anterior regions; but in forced breathing the sternum and ribs move together as if they were one solid piece. The lower portion of the chest and the epigastrium are retracted in inspiration; the costal angle is diminished, the ribs and cartilages connected with the sternum being sometimes on a line; the soft parts above the clavicle and sternum are often notably depressed with inspiration. Owing to depression of the heart downward and inward, the cardiac impulses are seen and felt in the epigastrium. Percussion and vocal resonance, at the same time, show the superficial cardiac region to be diminished or lost, the upper lobe of the left lung covering this space. There may be more or less anterior curvature of the spine, and the lower portions of the scapulæ may project, so that sometimes the plane of these bones is almost horizontal. These striking appearances characterize cases in which emphysema exists in a marked degree, and especially when the affection dates from early life. They are less marked or wanting if the emphysema be moderate in degree, and it have taken place in middle-aged persons or those advanced in years.

In the variety of emphysema distinguished as senile, or senile atrophy of the lungs, in which there is coalescence of air vesicles, from destruction of the cell walls, without increased volume of the affected lobes, the diagnosis is to be based on the vesiculo-tympanitic resonance on percussion, weakened respiratory murmur, with, perhaps, the alterations in rhythm, sinking of the soft parts above the clavicles, and the negative points, exclusive of deformity of the chest, which have been described.

Emphysema can hardly be confounded with any other affection than phthisis. The differentiation between these two affections is sufficiently easy, if the diagnostic points, positive and negative, of the former, be appreciated. Phthisis occurring in a patient affected with emphysema, makes a somewhat difficult problem in diagnosis, but, fortunately for the diagnostician, a patient with emphysema very rarely becomes phthisical.

Owing to the frequency with which an asthmatic element enters into the clinical history of emphysema, the dry bronchial (sibilant and sonorous) rales are often present, even when paroxysms of asthma do not occur.

Pleurisy, Acute and Chronic. Empyema. Hydrothorax.

In the first stage of acute pleurisy, that is, prior to the effusion of liquid, the physical conditions are, the presence of more or less recently exuded, soft, and glutinous lymph upon the pleural surfaces, which are now in contact, and restrained movements of respiration on the affected side in consequence of the pain which they occasion. In the second stage, serous liquid accumulates within the pleural cavity, the quantity varying in different cases, sometimes, although rarely, filling the chest on the affected side. In proportion to the quantity of liquid, the space over which the pleural surfaces are in contact is restricted, the movements of these surfaces over each other are limited, and the lung is condensed. In the third stage, the quantity of liquid decreases, the space over which the pleural surfaces are in contact increases, and the compressed lung is more or less expanded. The lymph upon the pleural surfaces becomes more dense and adherent. The surfaces may become agglutinated by the intervening lymph. Finally, in convalescence, permanent adhesions result from the production or growth of areolar tissue.

In subacute and chronic pleurisy, there is the same series of physical conditions, the points of difference being, as a rule, a less amount of exudation, and a greater amount of effused liquid. The quantity of liquid in chronic pleurisy is often sufficient to compress the lung into a small solid mass, situated at the upper and posterior part of the chest, and to dilate the affected side. The heart is often removed from its normal situation. If the pleurisy be on the left side, the heart may be pushed laterally beyond the right margin of the sternum; if the pleurisy be on the right side, the heart is pushed laterally to the left of its normal situation.

In empyema the accumulation of pus is apt to be still greater than that of serous effusion in simple chronic pleurisy, causing, of course, greater dilatation of the chest, and more displacement of the heart.

In these varieties of pleurisy, the affection, with rare exceptions, is unilateral.

In hydrothorax the conditions differ, *first,* as regards the absence of the exudation of lymph; *second,* the affection is bilateral, the effusion of liquid taking place in both pleural cavities; and *third,* although the quantity of liquid may be considerably greater on one side, the accumulation very rarely, if ever, is sufficient to cause much dilatation of the chest on that side, with complete condensation of the lung, and notable displacement of the heart.

The signs in the first stage of acute pleurisy are relative feebleness of the respiratory murmur on the affected side, from the restrained respiratory movements on that side, and a rubbing friction sound. The former is not distinctive of pleurisy, being present when the respiratory movements on one side are rest rained by pain in intercostal neuralgia and pleurodynia. A friction sound is not always obtained. In the absence of this sound, the physical diagnosis cannot be made with positiveness prior to the effusion of liquid. Assuming that the general and local symptoms point to an acute inflammatory affection, the differential diagnosis relates to pleurisy and pneumonia. A pleural friction sound may be present in the latter as well as the former of these two affections. The pathognomonic sign of pneumonia, the crepitant rale, being wanting, the differentiation, in this stage, must rest on diagnostic points pertaining to the symptoms.

In the second stage of acute pleurisy, the diagnostic signs are those which denote the presence of liquid within the pleural cavity. These signs are simple and distinctive. There is either dulness or flatness on percussion at the base of the chest, extending upward a distance proportionate to the quantity of liquid. If the trunk be in a vertical position, that is, the patient sitting or standing, the line of demarcation between the dulness or flatness and pulmonary resonance, is a horizontal line, on either the anterior, lateral, or posterior aspect of the chest. This line denotes the level of the liquid, and it is easily obtained by percussion. It is as easily determined by auscultating the vocal resonance, this either abruptly ceasing or being notably diminished at the level of the liquid. Having ascertained the horizontal line forming the upper boundary of dulness or flatness on the anterior aspect of the chest, the patient sitting or standing, if the position be changed to recumbency on the back, and the pulmonary resonance be found then to extend more or less below this line, this fact is demonstrative proof of the presence of liquid. Proof in this way is obtained in a large majority of cases, the exceptional cases being those in which the pleural surfaces are united, either by agglutination or permanent adhesions, above the level of the liquid. The resonance on percussion over the lung above the level of the liquid is generally vesiculo-tympanitic—the intensity increased, the pitch raised, the vesicular and tympanitic quality combined. Sometimes there is so little vesicular quality in this vesiculo-tympanitic resonance, that it may seem to be purely tympanitic, and is suggestive of pneumothorax. Associated signs will always prevent this error of observation. Vocal resonance and fremitus are either notably lessened or suppressed over the portion of the chest situated below the level of the liquid. The respiratory sound below the level of the liquid is suppressed. If any be heard, it is transmitted either from the lung above the liquid, or, laterally, from the lung on the other side of the chest. Above the liquid the respiratory sound, as a rule, is weakened. If the amount of liquid be sufficient to produce much condensation of lung, the respiratory sound is broncho-vesicular. Sometimes, owing to the pleural surfaces above being adherent, a strip of lung at the level of the liquid is sufficiently condensed by compression to give a bronchial respiration. Under these circumstances, there will be either bronchophony or the modification of that sign known as ægophony. If the lung be not sufficiently compressed for the production of these signs of solidification, the vocal resonance is simply more or less increased. The fremitus is usually increased above the liquid. Over the unaffected side the respiratory murmur is increased in intensity.

The foregoing signs are present when the pleural cavity is partially filled; a quarter, a half, or two-thirds of the thoracic space being occupied by liquid. The signs present when the cavity is completely filled, will be presently stated in connection with chronic pleurisy.

The signs which have been stated show not only the presence of liquid, but its quantity. By means of these signs are readily ascertained the progressive increase or decrease in the quantity of liquid, and its disappearance. After the liquid has disappeared, often notable dulness on percussion remains for some time, showing the presence of lymph not yet absorbed. During the decrease of the liquid, and after its disappearance, a friction murmur is often perceived. This murmur is now apt to be rough—a rasping, grating, or creaking sound. It may be loud enough to be heard by the patient, and by others at a distance from the chest. It continues sometimes for a considerable period.

The physical diagnosis in cases of chronic pleurisy, when the liquid occupies a portion only of the thoracic space, rests, of course, on precisely the same signs as in cases of acute pleurisy. If, however, the chest on the affected side be filled and dilated, certain of the signs which have been stated are wanting, and others are added. The affected side is everywhere flat on percussion. Flatness on percussion over the whole of one side, the affection being chronic, denotes, as a rule, with rare exceptions, either chronic simple pleurisy or empyema. Respiratory sound is wanting except at the summit over or near the compressed lung, where it is bronchial. Some cases offer an important exception to this rule, namely, the bronchial respiration is diffused over the greater part, or even the whole, of the affected side. The student should bear in mind this fact; otherwise, the diffusion of the bronchial respiration may lead to the suspicion that the flatness on percussion denotes solidification of lung, and not the presence of liquid. Other signs, however, should always correct this error. Vocal resonance and fremitus are either suppressed or notably diminished over the whole of the affected side. Generally, even when the chest is not dilated, the intercostal depressions are lessened or abolished. If the walls of the chest be thinly covered with integument, the two sides present a marked contrast in this respect. This is seen especially at the middle and lower regions of the chest anteriorly and laterally. It is especially marked at the end of the inspiratory act. If the affected side be dilated, this is apparent on inspection, and may be determined accurately by semicircular or diametric mensuration, callipers being required for the latter. The respiratory movements on the affected side are diminished or annulled, and they are increased on the healthy side, the two sides affording a marked contrast in this regard. If the pleurisy be on the left side, the impulses of the heart are not infrequently felt on the right of the sternum. If the impulses cannot be felt, auscultation shows the maximum of the intensity of the heart-sounds to be more or less removed to the right. If the pleurisy be on the right side, the impulses or sounds of the heart denote more or less displacement laterally to the left. The intensity of the respiratory murmur on the unaffected side is notably increased.

In cases of empyema the same signs are present as in chronic pleurisy. The character of the liquid does not alter appreciably any of the signs which have been stated. Dilatation of the affected side of the chest is more apt to occur, and to be more marked than in simple pleurisy. The differential diagnosis between these two varieties of pleurisy is to be made with positiveness by the introduction of a small trochar and obtaining enough of the liquid to ascertain its character.

When the left pleural cavity is filled with pus, the movements of the heart sometimes give to the affected side of the chest an impulse perceived by the eye and touch; hence, the term pulsating empyema. After a spontaneous perforation of the chest followed by a circumscribed purulent collection beneath the integument communicating with the pus within the pleural cavity, the tumor thus formed sometimes has a strong pulsation which is synchronous with the ventricular systole, and may give rise to the suspicion of aneurism.

In cases of hydrothorax the signs denote partial filling of the chest on both sides. The affection is bilateral. Generally the quantity of liquid in the two sides is not equal, and there is often a notable disparity in this respect. Friction sounds are never present. Variation of the level of the liquid with change of the position of the patient from the vertical to the horizontal, is nearly always determinable. Hydrothorax, meaning by this term a purely dropsical affection, is to be differentiated from double pleurisy with effusion. The history and symptoms, taken in connection with the signs, suffice for this discrimination.

Pneumothorax. Pneumo-hydrothorax.

In the extremely rare case of pneumothorax, that distinguished from pneumo-hydrothorax, the physical conditions are: the presence of air partially or completely occupying the thoracic space, and condensation of lung in proportion to the space occupied by air.

The diagnostic signs are, a purely tympanitic resonance over a portion or the whole of the affected side of the chest; suppression of the vesicular murmur over a space corresponding to that in which tympanitic resonance is obtained, with notable diminution or suppression of vocal resonance and fremitus. Over the compressed lung, if the condensation amount to complete or considerable solidification, there will be bronchial respiration and bronchophony; if the solidification be not complete nor considerable, there will be broncho-vesicular respiration with increased vocal resonance and fremitus. The accumulation of air may be sufficient to dilate the affected side, and to restrain or annul the respiratory movements on this side. The appearances on inspection are then precisely the same as in the cases of chronic pleurisy and empyema in which the affected side is dilated from the presence of liquid. Pneumothorax is, however, at once differentiated by the tympanitic resonance on percussion. If one side of the chest be more or less dilated, and the resonance over the side be purely tympanitic, the thoracic space must be filled, not with liquid, but with air. The intensity of the respiratory murmur on the healthy side is increased.

In the great majority of cases in which the pleural cavity contains air, there is also present more or less liquid, which may be serous or purulent. The affection is then known as pneumo-hydrothorax. The physical conditions are the same as in pneumothorax, with the exception of the presence of liquid. The relative proportions of liquid and air in different cases are variable, and, also, in the same case at different periods.

The physical diagnosis of pneumo-hydrothorax, as distinguished from pneumothorax, embraces the signs of liquid, in addition to those of air, within the pleural cavity. If the quantity of liquid be large or considerable, percussion at the base of the chest gives flatness extending upward more or less, and tympanitic resonance above, the patient either sitting or standing. The upper limit of flatness when the body is vertical is bounded by a horizontal line on the anterior, or lateral, or posterior aspect of the chest. A change from the vertical to the horizontal position invariably causes variation of the upper limit of the flatness, inasmuch as the liquid and air change their relative situations without an exception. The quantity of liquid is determined approximately by ascertaining the space over which the flatness on percussion extends. The line which divides the flatness and the tympanitic resonance does not accurately denote the level of the liquid, because tympanitic resonance is transmitted a certain distance below this level; hence, it is always to be assumed that the level of the liquid is somewhat higher than the upper boundary of the flatness.

In both pneumothorax and pneumo-hydrothorax a group of auscultatory signs are often found which are highly diagnostic, indeed almost pathognomonic. These signs are amphoric respiration, amphoric voice or echo, and metallic tinkling. The amphoric and the tinkling sounds may be present, either without the other, but they are not infrequently associated. Neither are present in every case, and they are not present in the same case at all times; their absence, therefore, by no means excludes the affections, and they are not essential to the diagnosis. When present, they denote either air or air and liquid in the pleural cavity with perforation of lung, or a large phthisical cavity. Their occurrence in the latter is extremely rare, and, whenever they are associated with other signs already stated, their diagnostic import is demonstrative.

Pneumo-hydrothorax may almost invariably be diagnosticated instantly by the presence of a succussion sound. Whenever distinct splashing is produced by percussion and referable to the chest, that is, not produced within the stomach, it is demonstrative of the presence of air and liquid within the pleural cavity.

Acute Lobar Pneumonia.

In the first stage of this disease, there is an abnormal accumulation of blood within the vessels of the affected lobe (active congestion or hyperæmia), with some glutinous exudation within the air vesicles and bronchioles. Generally some exuded lymph is upon the pleural surface, this being due to circumscribed dry pleurisy. In most cases there is also circumscribed bronchitis, which is limited to the tubes within the affected lobe. In the second stage, there is solidification, due to fibrinous exudation within the air vesicles. The solidification, at first limited, extends either rapidly or slowly, as a rule, over the whole lobe. Exceptionally, more or less liquid effusion into the pleural cavity takes place (pleuro-pneumonia), the pleurisy then extending beyond the limits of the affected lobe. In this stage the pneumonia may involve either another lobe of the lung primarily affected, or a lobe of the opposite lung; and sometimes the affection, by successive invasions, extends over the whole of one lung, together with a lobe of the opposite lung. The pneumonia, in these secondary invasions, is usually accompanied by pleurisy and bronchitis. In the stage of resolution, the solidification of the affected lobe, or lobes, decreases, sometimes rapidly and sometimes slowly, until the normal condition is restored. If resolution do not take place, and the affection pass into the stage of purulent infiltration, the air vesicles and bronchial tubes contain a puruloid liquid in greater or less quantity. Exceptionally pus is collected in a cavity, or in cavities, constituting pulmonary abscess.

The physical diagnosis of acute lobar pneumonia in the first stage, must be based on the presence of the crepitant rale, with moderate or slight dulness on percussion over the affected lobe. There is sometimes in this stage a pleuritic rubbing sound over the affected lobe. The crepitant rale is not always present, and, hence, the affection cannot be excluded by the absence of this sign. When present, taken in connection with the symptoms, this sign is pathognomonic of the affection. It is important not to mistake for this sign fine bubbling or the subcrepitant rale. When the crepitant rale is wanting, a positive physical diagnosis must be deferred until more or less of the affected lobe becomes solidified, that is, when the affection passes into the second stage.

The diagnosis in the second stage is to be based on the signs of solidification furnished by auscultation and percussion. The auscultatory signs are the broncho-vesicular, followed by the bronchial, respiration; increased vocal resonance, followed by bronchophony, and increased bronchial whisper, followed by whispering bronchophony. The signs of solidification are manifest at first within a circumscribed space, situated over either the upper, the lower, or the middle portion of the affected lobe; and either rapidly or slowly the signs extend, in most cases, over the entire lobe. The crepitant rale, if it have been present in the first, generally disappears in the second stage. Sometimes, however, it is not entirely lost in this stage. The broncho-vesicular respiration, increased vocal resonance, and increased bronchial whisper are present when the solidification is slight or moderate; the bronchial respiration, bronchophony, and bronchophonic whisper take their place when the solidification becomes considerable or complete. The latter signs, as a rule, speedily follow, inasmuch as the solidification in most cases quickly becomes complete or considerable. The foregoing three signs, denoting considerable or complete solidification, are usually present. Bronchial respiration, however, is sometimes present without bronchophony, and ***vice versa.*** Either, present alone, suffices to show the existence and the extent of the solidification. Moist bronchial or bubbling rales are sometimes, but rarely, heard over the affected lobe.

There is notable dulness on percussion in the second stage. The dulness may approximate, and even amount to flatness. If a single lobe be affected, the dulness, or flatness, extends over a space corresponding to that occupied by the lobe or the portion of it which is solidified. In the antero-lateral aspects of the chest, the dividing line between the solidified and the healthy lobe is readily ascertained by percussion, and this line is coincident with the interlobar fissure. It sometimes happens that the upper and the lower lobe of the right lung are affected, the middle lobe not becoming involved. The space corresponding to the middle lobe may then form an island of resonance surrounded by notable dulness on percussion.

Whenever one lobe of a lung is affected, the resonance over the unaffected part of the same lung is abnormally increased, the pitch is raised, and the quality is vesiculo-tympanitic; vesiculo-tympanitic resonance, in other words, is produced. This renders more marked the contrast between dulness over the solidified, and resonance over the healthy, lobe.

Over a portion of an upper lobe in the second stage, instead of notable dulness or flatness, there may be marked tympanitic resonance. This resonance proceeds from air within the trachea, and the bronchi exterior to the lungs, the lung-substance being completely solidified; it is chiefly or especially marked over the site of these air tubes. In some cases the tympanitic resonance has the cracked-metal or the amphoric intonation. These signs, *per se,* might suggest either pneumothorax or phthisical cavities; the associated respiratory and vocal signs, however, show only solidification of lung. In cases of pneumonia affecting the left lung, a tympanitic resonance is not infrequently propagated from the stomach more or less upward over the affected side of the chest. This may be readily traced to the stomach. On the right side, a tympanitic resonance is sometimes propagated, a certain distance upward, from the transverse colon.

The commencement of the stage of resolution is denoted by a broncho-vesicular respiration. The first change observed is the presence of a little vesicular quality in the inspiratory sound. When this is observed, the respiration is no longer bronchial, but has become broncho-vesicular, although the pitch is still high, and the expiration is prolonged, high, tubular. This slight change shows that air begins to enter the pulmonary vesicles. As resolution goes on, more and more of the vesicular takes the place of the tubular quality in the inspiratory sound, and the pitch is lowered in proportion; the expiratory sound becomes proportionately less and less prolonged, its pitch lowered, its quality less tubular, until, at length, the normal characters of the respiratory murmur are regained. Resolution is then complete.

While the broncho-vesicular respiration is undergoing the modifications just stated, the vocal sounds have corresponding changes. Bronchophony persists for some time after the respiration has become broncho-vesicular, and then disappears, increased vocal resonance generally taking its place, and persisting until resolution is completed. The bronchial whisper loses its bronchophonic characters, and is simply increased until its normal characters are regained. While the solidification is complete, the vocal fremitus may, or may not, be increased. It is sometimes diminished. When, however, resolution has so far progressed that bronchophony is lost, the fremitus is usually greater than in health, and so continues, but progressively lessening until the solidification entirely disappears.

During the progress of resolution, the dulness on percussion diminishes in proportion as air enters the air vesicles. If tympanitic resonance have been present over the upper lobe, this gives place to a vesicular resonance. Some dulness, however, remains after the completion of resolution, and persists until the exuded lymph on the pleural surface is absorbed. The amount of dulness remaining when the respiratory and vocal signs denote resolution, is proportionate to the quantity of exudation incident to the associated pleurisy.

In this stage the crepitant rale not infrequently returns, if it have entirely disappeared during the second stage, and if it have persisted, it is more marked and diffused. It is now known as the returning crepitant rale. More frequently the rale in this stage is a fine bubbling or the subcrepitant. Both rales are not infrequently associated; and, from the distinctive characters of each, they are readily distinguished. Moist rales more or less fine or coarse are not infrequent.

If the affection pass into the stage of purulent infiltration, the respiratory sounds are feeble or suppressed, having, if present, more or less of the bronchial characters. Babbling bronchial rales, coarse and fine, are abundant. Weak bronchophony may persist, or the vocal resonance may be diminished. Fremitus may, or may not, be increased. Notable dulness or flatness on percussion remains.

If the pneumonia result in pulmonic abscess, there will be notable dulness or flatness on percussion within a circumscribed space, together with absence of respiratory murmur, and diminished or suppressed vocal resonance. These signs warrant a probable diagnosis which is corroborated by the sudden expectoration of pus in a considerable quantity. The signs just stated may then be followed by those denoting a cavity, namely, cavernous respiration and whisper, with intense vocal resonance.

Circumscribed Pneumonia. Embolic Pneumonia.

Hemorrhagic Infarctus or Pulmonary Apoplexy.

The form of pneumonia known as lobular pneumonia, occurring chiefly in children, has been considered (*vide* Bronchitis seated in small-sized tubes). Whenever circumscribed, as a rule, pneumonia is secondary to some other pulmonary affection. Circumscribed pneumonia, having the anatomical characters of acute lobar pneumonia, that is, giving rise to an intra-vesicular exudation which may disappear readily by resolution or absorption, is not infrequent in cases of phthisis. The signs are those which represent solidification of lung within an area more or less circumscribed; but the differentiation from the solidification proper to phthisis (tuberculous pneumonia), can only be made with positiveness after the signs have showed that the solidification has notably diminished or disappeared.

In embolic pneumonia, followed by what has been known as metastatic abscesses, there may be dulness on percussion, with feeble bronchial or bronchovesicular respiration, or suppression of respiratory sound, weak bronchophony or increase of vocal resonance, within a circumscribed space, or spaces, generally on the posterior aspect of the chest, and oftenest on the right side. These signs, taken in connection with the symptoms and pathological conditions which are consistent with the supposition of infectious emboli received into the right side of the heart, namely, when the pulmonary symptoms follow puerperal disease, ulcers, wounds, or injuries, render the diagnosis quite positive. If, however, the pulmonary affection consist of small disseminated nodules, the foregoing signs will not be present. The diagnosis then must be based on the history and symptoms, taken in connection with the exclusion of other pulmonary affections by the absence of signs which should be present if they existed. Bubbling rales at different situations may indicate the probable sites of the nodules. There may be pleuritic friction sounds. The signs may show, as a complication, pleurisy with effusion.

Extravasation of blood (pneumorrhagia), if it be in small spaces, gives rise to no definite physical signs. If, however, extravasation extend over a considerable space, there will be dulness on percussion, with feeble or suppressed respiratory sound within an area corresponding to the extent of the extravasation. Within and near this area there will be likely to be moist bronchial rales more or less fine or coarse. The signs of solidification will not be present if the extravasation be unaccompanied by pneumonia.

Pulmonary Gangrene.

In diffused pulmonary gangrene, the physical signs are those of solidification extending over the greater part or the whole of a lobe. The diagnosis, however, can only be made when, in connection with these signs, there are present the characteristic fœtor of the breath and expectoration.

In circumscribed gangrene there is dulness or flatness on percussion within an area corresponding to the extent of the affection, with either suppression of respiratory sound, or bronchial respiration, and the vocal signs of solidification. Within and near this space moist bronchial rales are likely to be heard. The situation is usually on the posterior aspect of the chest. These signs do not suffice for a positive diagnosis, without the characteristic breath and expectoration. Cavernous signs may appear after the gangrenous portion of lung has sloughed away, and been expectorated.

Pulmonary Œdema.

The physical condition expressed by the term pulmonary œdema is the presence of effused serum within the air vesicles. With this condition is associated more or less pulmonary congestion.

In cases of pulmonary œdema developed rapidly and largely in connection with renal disease, with obstruction at the mitral orifice of the heart, or with both these affections combined, giving rise to great dyspnœa, and liable to end speedily in death, the following are the diagnostic signs: dulness or percussion on both sides of the chest, especially over the lower lobes, fine bubbling or the subcrepitant rale diffused over the chest on both sides, together with coarser bubbling sounds, and the murmur of respiration notably weak or suppressed over the lower lobes. Inasmuch as the lungs are not solidified, the rales are low in pitch. The vocal signs of solidification are, of course, wanting. Occasionally the crepitant rale is mingled with the fine bubbling sounds.

This form of the affection is to be differentiated from hydrothorax with large effusion, and from so-called capillary bronchitis. Hydrothorax is always associated with more or less anasarca or general dropsy, whereas, pulmonary œdema, even when dependent on renal disease, may occur without dropsical effusion elsewhere. Moreover, the presence of liquid within the pleural cavities, and its amount, may always be determined demonstratively in cases of hydrothorax (*vide* Pleurisy with Effusion and Hydrothorax). Capillary bronchitis occurs chiefly in children. The subcrepitant rale on both sides of the chest is the diagnostic sign of this affection; but it is not accompanied by dulness on percussion except in so far as the bronchitis may be associated with lobular pneumonia or collapse of pulmonary lobules. The rapid development of the œdema and its pathological connections, are diagnostic points to be taken into account.

Pneumonia is excluded by the fact that the affection is at the beginning bilateral, and by the absence of the signs of solidification of lung.

Pulmonary œdema less in degree and diffusion has, of course, the same signs, not as marked and not as extensive, namely, dulness on percussion and fine bubbling sounds or the subcrepitant rale. In this form the affection is bilateral, and seated especially in the posterior and inferior portions of the lungs. Moreover, this form has the same pathological connections, namely, with disease of the kidneys, and mitral lesions of the heart. The low pitch of the bronchial rales, and the absence of the respiratory and vocal signs of solidification, together with the fact of the affection being bilateral, and the coexistence of disease of the heart or kidneys, constitute the basis of a positive diagnosis.

Hypostatic congestion of the lungs may occasion a certain amount of pulmonary œdema. The physical diagnosis is to be based on bilateral dulness on the posterior aspect of the chest, with low-pitched fine bubbling sounds or the subcrepitant rale on both sides, these signs occurring under circumstances which lead to the supposition of this form of congestion.

Carcinoma of Lung. Tumors within the Chest.

Carcinomatous growths in the lungs are usually in the form of nodules varying in size from that of a pea to a hen's egg, disseminated throughout one lung or both lungs in greater or less numbers. These disseminated nodules, if of small size, have no well-marked, definite diagnostic signs. If limited to a lung, or if more numerous in one lung, they may occasion an appreciable dulness on percussion. They may also occasion feebleness of the respiratory murmur, and, owing to coexisting circumscribed bronchitis, moist bronchial rales may be heard at different points. These signs warrant a diagnosis when, as is usually the case, cancer is known to have existed elsewhere. With reference to diagnosis, it is to be borne in mind that, when cancer of the lung is secondary, both lungs are affected, and, when it is primary, the affection is generally unilateral.

If there be nodules of considerable size, there will be well-marked dulness on percussion in different situations, and the signs of solidification may be present, namely, bronchial or broncho-vesicular respiration, increased vocal resonance or bronchophony, and increased vocal fremitus.

In some cases of unilateral carcinoma, the greater part, or the whole, of a lung may be infiltrated with the morbid growth, increasing its volume and giving rise to enlargement of the affected side, diminished respiratory movements or immobility, flatness on percussion with diminished or suppressed respiratory murmur, vocal resonance, and fremitus. If, as is usual, there be also more or less pleuritic effusion, the intercostal spaces may be pushed out to a level with the ribs. Here are the signs which denote chronic pleurisy with large effusion, and the differential diagnosis cannot be made with positiveness until the fluid within the chest be withdrawn, and it be found that, irrespective of the bulging of the intercostal spaces, the physical signs remain. Exploration with a small trochar will settle the diagnosis when then is no pleuritic effusion, and this procedure is unobjectionable.

In other cases the carcinomatous growth induces atrophy of the lung, diminishing its volume, and causing notable contraction of the affected side. The appearances on inspection are those which denote contraction after chronic pleurisy, and which may be present also in cases of cirrhosis of lung. The differential diagnosis must be based chiefly on diagnostic points relating to the history and symptoms.

Tumors within the chest, generally having their points of departure in the mediastinum, displace the lung in proportion to their size. They may cause considerable displacement of the heart, and produce more or less enlargement of the chest with diminished respiratory movements. Over the site of the tumor, there will be dulness or flatness on percussion. Generally respiratory sound is wanting, vocal resonance and fremitus being either diminished or suppressed. In the neighborhood of the primary bronchi and over lung compressed by the tumor, there may be bronchial respiration, with bronchophony and increased fremitus. If the chest be enlarged, its enlargement is not likely to be as uniform as when it is dilated with liquid; this is a diagnostic point. The tumor, or the tumors, may not be confined to one side of the chest. It is to be borne in mind that pleurisy with effusion may exist as a complication, and this may serve to obscure the diagnosis.

The physical diagnosis involves differentiation from pericarditis with effusion and aneurisms. These affections are to be excluded by the absence of their diagnostic signs.

Acute Miliary Tuberculosis.

The physical condition in this affection is the presence of a large number of the small bodies known as tubercles or miliary granulations disseminated throughout both lungs. Bronchitis is an associated affection.

If the tubercles be about equally distributed in the two lungs, there is no abnormal disparity of the resonance on percussion between the two sides of the chest. A comparison, also, of the two sides may afford no disparity as regards the respiratory murmur, vocal resonance, and fremitus. Moist rales, due to the associated bronchitis, may be present in different situations. A physical diagnosis, under these circumstances, cannot be made with positiveness. Physical exploration, however, is important, in order to exclude other affections; and the negative result, taken in connection with the symptoms—hyperpyrexia, rapid pulse, accelerated breathing, etc.—renders the diagnosis extremely probable. The differential diagnosis involves discrimination from capillary bronchitis, and an essential fever with a bronchial complication. The affection has been repeatedly mistaken for typhoid fever.

The tubercles may be more abundantly distributed in one lung. A disparity in the resonance on percussion may then be apparent, and, perhaps, an abnormal increase of vocal resonance and fremitus. These signs, taken in connection with the symptoms, establish the physical diagnosis.

Phthisis.

With reference to physical diagnosis, cases of phthisis may be conveniently distributed into three groups, as follows: 1st. Cases in which the pulmonary affection is small, or cases of incipient phthisis; 2d. Cases in which the affection is moderate or considerable; and 3d. Cases in which the affection has progressed to the formation of cavities, or cases of advanced phthisis.

In cases of incipient phthisis, the essential physical condition is the presence of small solidified masses, or nodules, the intervening vesicular structure not being affected. These nodules vary from the size of a pea to a filbert. In the vast majority of cases they are situated at or near the apex of either the right or the left lung. Generally, circumscribed capillary bronchitis coexists in proximity to the nodules. An intercurrent circumscribed ordinary pneumonia sometimes occurs, giving rise to transient solidification within a limited area. Dry circumscribed pleurisy, situated over the affected portion of lung, generally occurs from time to time.

In the cases of a moderate or a considerable pulmonary affection, the difference, as compared with the preceding group of cases, consists in the presence of nodules of larger size, or solidification from the phthisical deposit extending over a space, or spaces, sufficient in size to give rise to well-marked physical signs. The solidification in these cases may be extended by the development of circumscribed interstitial pneumonia. The circumscribed bronchitis is greater, as a rule, in degree and extent; attacks of dry pleurisy may continue to occur, and the pleural surfaces become adherent. In these cases, generally, the affection, existing primarily in one lung, now exists in both lungs. The volume of the lung first affected, at the summit, is more or less diminished. Enlargement of the bronchial glands is usual, and these may be so situated as to press upon and diminish the calibre of one of the primary bronchi. In some cases, portions of lung in the neighborhood of solidified masses or nodules are emphysematous (lobular emphysema).

Cases of advanced phthisis are characterized by the presence of a cavity, or, commonly, of cavities, varying in number, size, rigidity or flaccidity of the walls, freedom of communication with bronchial tubes, and their situation relatively to the superficies of the lung. In cases of progressive phthisis, in addition to cavities, there is more or less solidification from phthisical exudation and interstitial pneumonia. The volume of the lung at the summit is often notably diminished. The pleural surfaces are firmly adherent. If, however, the disease has been retrogressive, there may be little or no solidification of lung, the cavity or cavities forming the only lesion. In cases of advanced phthisis, with very rare exceptions, both lungs are affected, and cavities often exist on both sides.

The physical diagnosis in cases of incipient phthisis embraces what may be called direct and accessory signs. The accessory signs are those which represent incidental affections, namely, circumscribed bronchitis, pleurisy, and pneumonia. The direct signs are those representing the essential condition, namely, the solidified masses or nodules.

An important direct sign is dulness on percussion. Slight dulness on percussion at the summit of the chest, in front or behind, is a highly important sign, taken in connection with symptoms, of incipient phthisis. In determining that a relative dulness is abnormal, the student must bear in mind, in the first place, the normal disparity between the two sides. The right side at the summit is relatively somewhat dull on percussion in healthy persons. Due allowance is to be made for this normal disparity. In the second place, it is to be borne in mind that any deformity affecting the symmetry of the chest will affect the relative resonance on the two sides; and that a deviation from symmetry attributable to the position of the patient will occasion a disparity on percussion. In the third place, the rules for the practice of percussion must be kept in mind, in order to avoid producing a disparity by the non-observance of these rules (*vide* p. 54). Normal resonance on percussion on the two sides is a strong point for the exclusion of incipient phthisis.

The direct respiratory signs in incipient phthisis are the broncho-vesicular respiration and weakened vesicular murmur. Of course, familiarity with the characters of the broncho-vesicular respiration is indispensable—the combination of the vesicular and the tubular quality in the inspiratory sound, with the pitch raised in proportion to the amount of tubularity, and the expiratory sound more or less prolonged, high, and tubular. Not infrequently the only appreciable morbid modification is diminished intensity of the murmur. When this sign is present, it is probable that the lack of intensity is the reason for the absence of the characters of the broncho-vesicular modifications; that is, the latter sign would have been present were the respiratory sounds more intense.

The direct vocal signs in incipient phthisis are, increased vocal resonance, increased bronchial whisper, and increased fremitus. The other direct signs may be present, without an appreciable morbid increase of the vocal resonance or fremitus. The increased whisper may also be wanting, but more rarely than the two other vocal signs.

In deciding on the presence or absence of each and all of these direct signs, it is essential to know and to judge correctly of the disparity between the two sides of the chest at the summit in health. Normally, the resonance on percussion at the summit on the right side is slightly dull as compared with the left side; the inspiratory sound on this side has some tubularity in quality, and is somewhat raised in pitch; the expiratory sound may be more or less prolonged, high, and tubular; the vocal resonance, on the right side, is always greater, the same being true of fremitus; the bronchial whisper is louder on the right side, and the intensity of the respiratory murmur is a little less on this side. Whenever it is a question as to a small phthisical affection at or near the apex of the right lung, it is a matter of experience and judgment to decide if the disparity in respect of these points be greater than normal; and it is not always easy to come at once to a decision. From the want of a proper appreciation of the several points of disparity in health, it is not uncommon for an erroneous diagnosis of phthisis to be based thereon. Appreciating the normal points of disparity, it is obviously easier to determine that the several direct signs of incipient phthisis are present at the left, than at the right, summit; relative dulness on percussion, broncho-vesicular or weakened respiration, increased vocal resonance, whisper, and fremitus, at the left summit, are, of course, always abnormal.

In connection with the foregoing direct signs may be mentioned another sign which is often available, namely, an abnormal transmission of the heart-sounds. This sign is available only in the central portion of the infra-clavicular region. A slight degree of solidification of the summit of one lung renders the heart-sounds more audible in the situation just named. It is of assistance in determining this sign, to be familiar with the following points of disparity which exist in health: on the right side the second sound of the heart is somewhat more audible than on the left side, and on the left side the first sound is a little louder than on the right side. Hence, if the first sound be better conducted on the right than on the left side, it is abnormal; and if the second sound be louder on the left side, it is abnormal. This sign is always to be taken in connection with other direct signs; it gives greater diagnostic strength to the latter, but it is by no means, in itself, sufficient for the diagnosis.

Corroborative evidence of incipient phthisis may be obtained by the presence of accessory signs. These are, *first*, fine bubbling or the subcrepitant rale at the summit on one side. This sign denotes a circumscribed capillary bronchitis, and this, at the summit on one side, is usually associated with phthisis. **Second,** a crepitant rale at the summit on one side denotes a circumscribed pneumonia which is usually secondary to phthisis. **Third,** a pleuritic friction sound limited to the summit on one side is evidence of a dry circumscribed pleurisy which occurs often in the early stage of phthisis. **Fourth,** indeterminate rales, crumpling, and crackling, are significant of phthisis if limited to the summit on one side. These rales, it is to be recollected, are sometimes found in healthy persons on forced breathing, especially if the binaural stethoscope be employed. If they be normal they are found on both sides. The accessory signs are not sufficient for a positive diagnosis if they exist alone; but they are to be considered as corroborating evidence derived from the direct signs, together with the symptoms and history.

As regards differential diagnosis, the affections with which incipient phthisis are likely to be confounded, are chronic bronchitis, and moderate emphysema. With respect to the first of these affections, namely, chronic bronchitis, the differentiation must depend on the presence or the absence of positive signs of phthisis; in other words, phthisis is either diagnosticated or excluded. The physical signs in cases of moderate emphysema sometimes lead to the error of supposing this affection to be phthisis. Owing to the relatively greater intensity of the resonance on percussion at the left summit, dulness is thought to exist at the right summit, and a prolonged expiration, with the normally greater vocal resonance at the right summit, are set down as signs of phthisis. This error may be avoided by a careful study of the signs of emphysema and the normal disparity in respiration, vocal resonance, and fremitus, existing between the two sides of the chest.

The physical diagnosis of a phthisical affection which is considerable or moderate in amount, is, in most cases, an easy problem. Inspection often furnishes marked signs. The upper anterior portion of the chest on one side is depressed or flattened, and the superior costal movements of respiration are diminished, the chest elsewhere being symmetrical in both size and motions. There is more or less marked dulness on percussion at the upper part of the chest on the affected side. Sometimes the diminished resonance is tympanitic in quality (tympanitic dulness) without the existence of cavities, the resonance being conducted from the primary and secondary bronchial tubes. The respiration is bronchial, or broncho-vesicular approximating more or less to the bronchial. Occasionally, however, the respiratory sounds are too feeble for their characters to be appreciated. There is bronchophony, or the vocal resonance is notably increased without the bronchophonic characters. The whisper is either distinctly bronchophonic or it is notably increased in intensity, high in pitch, and tubular in quality. Vocal fremitus is often increased. Moist bronchial rales, coarse or fine, are generally present. With these diagnostic signs on one side, the signs of a smaller amount of disease are generally present on the other side.

In some cases of a moderate phthisical affection, the judgment may be confused by the resonance on percussion being increased or vesiculo-tympanitic on the affected side. This sign denotes the coexistence of lobular emphysema developed in the progress of phthisis. The diagnosis of the latter affection is then to be based on the signs obtained by auscultation.

In advanced phthisis the physical diagnosis of the disease is sufficiently easy. The signs distinctive of this stage of the disease are those which denote pulmonary cavities, namely, tympanitic resonance on percussion within a circumscribed space; cracked metal or amphoric resonance; cavernous respiration; cavernous whisper and sometimes pectoriloquy; amphoric respiration and voice, and gurgling (*vide* Chapter V. for descriptions of these signs).

The cavernous signs are generally associated with the signs of solidification. In some cases, however, in which the disease has been non-progressive and retrogressive, the cavernous signs are present without the signs which denote solidification of lung.

Fibroid Phthisis, Interstitial Pneumonia, or Cirrhosis of Lung.

In this affection the physical conditions are, solidification from hyperplasia of the interstitial pulmonary tissue, dilatation of bronchial tubes (bronchiectasis) and diminished volume of the lung affected. The affection, as a rule, is limited to one side. The whole of a lung, or only a portion of it, may be affected. Bronchitis always coexists.

There is notable dulness on percussion, the diminished resonance being sometimes tympanitic. The degree of resonance may vary at different examinations, owing to differences in the amount of morbid products within the bronchial tubes. The respiration is bronchial, or broncho-vesicular. At times from obstruction of

affected side of the chest becomes contracted either entirely or in part, resembling in this respect the appearances after chronic pleurisy.

With these signs the affection is to be differentiated from the ordinary form of phthisis, by reference to points pertaining to the symptoms and history.

Diaphragmatic Hernia.

The presence of more or less of the hollow abdominal viscera within the thoracic cavity in consequence of a congenital deficiency of a portion of the diaphragm, or perforation from accidents, or enlargement of the natural openings, gives rise to certain anomalous signs, namely, a tympanitic resonance, variable at different times owing to differences as regards the quantity of gas within the viscera; absence of the respiratory murmur from the base of the chest upward, the height proportional to the space occupied by the abdominal organs, and the intestinal sounds emanating from within the chest, not conducted from below.

This extremely rare affection can only be confounded with pneumothorax. The latter affection is to be excluded by the absence of its diagnostic signs, irrespective of the tympanitic resonance on percussion.

CHAPTER VII.
THE PHYSICAL CONDITIONS OF THE HEART IN HEALTH AND DISEASE.
THE HEAHT-SOUNDS AND CARDIAC MURMURS.

Physical conditions of the heart in health:—Boundaries of the præcordia—Normal situation of the apex-beat—Boundaries of the deep and of the superficial cardiac space—Relations of the aorta and the pulmonary artery to the walls of the chest—The heart-sounds—Characters distinguishing the first and the second sound—Mechanism of the production of the heart-sounds—Auscultation of the pulmonic and the aortic second sound separately—Movements of the auricles and ventricles in relation to each other—Physical conditions of the heart in disease:—Enlargement of the heart—Hypertrophy and dilatation—Abnormal impulses of the heart, and modifications of the apex-beat—Valvular lesions—Roughness of the pericardial surfaces—Liquid within the pericardial sac—Abnormal modifications of the heart-sounds—Reduplication of heart-sounds—Cardiac murmurs—Normal and abnormal blood-currents within the heart, and their relations with the heart-sounds—Mitral direct murmur—Mitral regurgitant murmur—Mitral systolic non-regurgitant, or intra-ventricular murmur—Aortic direct murmur—Aortic regurgitant murmur, and an aortic diastolic non-regurgitant murmur—Coexisting endocardial murmurs—Tricuspid direct murmur—Tricuspid regurgitant murmur—Pulmonic direct murmur—Pulmonic regurgitant murmur—Facts of practical importance in relation to endocardial murmurs—Pericardial or friction murmur.

BEFORE entering upon the study of the physical diagnosis of the diseases of the heart, the student must be familiar with its anatomy and physiology. For a description of the structure and functions of this organ, he is referred to anatomical and physiological treatises. The plan of this work embraces the anatomical relations of the heart and the space which it occupies within the chest, as physical conditions of health determinable by normal signs, together with the heart-sounds. Having briefly stated these conditions of health, the morbid physical conditions which may be ascertained by percussion, auscultation, and other methods of physical exploration, will be considered. The latter heading will include an account of the cardiac murmurs.

The Physical Conditions of the Heart in Health.

The Præcordia. The Superficial and the Deep Cardiac Space.—The area on the surface of the chest corresponding to the space which the heart occupies within the chest, is the præcordial region, or the præcordia. The upper, lower, and two lateral boundaries of this region must be memorized. The upper boundary is the third rib, the lower is a horizontal line passing through the fifth intercostal space; the left lateral boundary is at, or a little within, a vertical line passing through the nipple, the *linea mammalis,* and the right lateral boundary is represented by a vertical line situated about a finger's breadth to the right of the right margin of the sternum. As the volume of the heart varies, within certain limits, in different healthy persons, the boundaries of the præcordia are, of course, not always exactly the same. The foregoing statements are sufficiently accurate for practical purposes.

The horizontal line representing the lower boundary of the præcordia, intersects the point where the apex-beat of the heart is felt. The normal situation of the apex-beat must be recollected. In most healthy persons the apex-beat is felt in the fifth intercostal space a little within the linea mammalis. This is, assuming the persons to be sitting or standing; in recumbency on the back the beat something rises to the fourth intercostal space, and it is sometimes found in the fourth space in the sitting or standing position of the body. The distance from the linea mammalis varies in different healthy persons; it is sufficiently accurate to say it is a little within that line. The force of the apex-beat varies much in different healthy persons, owing to other causes than the power of the heart's action, such as the amount of muscular substance and fat in that situation, the width of the intercostal space, the convexity of the chest, the relation to the left lung, etc. Allowance is to be made for these variations in determining the abnormal modifications of the force of the beat, which belong among the physical signs of disease.

Within a portion of the præcordia the heart is uncovered of lung, and in the remaining portion lung intervenes between the heart and the walls of the chest. The former of these portions is called the superficial, and the latter is called the deep cardiac space. The deep cardiac space on the right side extends to the median line. On the left side the lung recedes at a point on the median line on a level with the cartilage of the fourth rib, and the anterior border of the upper lobe makes an outward curve, returning inward at or near the apex of the heart. This leaves the heart uncovered within an area which, for practical purposes, may be represented by a right-angled triangle, the hypothenuse extending from the median line on a level with the costal cartilage of the fourth rib to the apex of the heart; the right angle formed by the median line and the horizontal line which forms the lower boundary of the præcordia.

The limits of the superficial cardiac space may be easily defined by percussion. It is only necessary to ascertain the curved line formed by the receding anterior border of the upper lobe of the left lung. A distinct, although not great, dulness on percussion marks this border of the lung. The border of the lung is as distinctly marked by the abrupt diminution of the vocal resonance, if auscultation be made with the stethoscope. The outer boundaries of the deep cardiac space may also be determined by percussion; distinct, although slight, dulness marks the limits of the præcordia. Defining thus the boundaries of the præcordia and of the superficial cardiac space in healthy persons, makes a good practical exercise in percussion.

Relations of the Aorta and Pulmonary Artery to the Walls of the Chest.—The base of the heart, especially in connection with auscultatory signs, is generally considered to be at the second intercostal space near the sternum, this situation being, in reality, just above the base. In this situation sounds produced at the aortic and the pulmonic orifice are best studied, either in health or disease. With reference to these sounds, the anatomical relations of the aorta and the pulmonary artery to the right and the left second intercostal space are of importance. If the stethoscope be applied in the second intercostal space on the right side, close to the sternum, it is very near the aorta, and sounds produced at the aortic orifice are best heard in this situation. If the stethoscope be applied in the second intercostal space on the left side, it is very near the pulmonary artery, and the sounds produced at the pulmonic orifice are best heard in this situation. Reference will be made to these two situations in giving an account of the heart-sounds in health and disease, and of adventitious sounds or murmurs.

The Heart-sounds.—The characters which distinguish, respectively, the first and the second sound of the heart are to be studied preparatory to the study of the abnormal modifications which are important physical signs of disease. It is essential also to be able always to make the distinction practically between the first and the second sound in order to connect with each sound separately cardiac murmurs. The conventional sense of the term heart-sounds, as distinguished from cardiac murmurs, must be borne in mind. The cardiac murmurs are adventitious sounds; they are never merely abnormal modifications of the heart-sounds, but they are new sounds added to these.

The two heart-sounds follow in a certain rhythmical order, and, in health, this suffices for the recognition of each. It answers all practical purposes to say that the first and the second sound follow each other after an interval which is just appreciable, this interval being the short pause of the heart. After the two sounds an interval is readily appreciable, called the long pause of the heart. It is not necessary to carry in the memory the exact relative duration of each of the sounds and each of the intervals. The fractions of a unit, in fact, do not express the length of the sounds and intervals as correctly as less definite expressions, inasmuch as the figures represent only the mean of variations within the limits of health. It is sufficiently definite to say that, with the ear or stethoscope applied over the situation of the apex-beat, the first sound is longer than the second, louder, lower in pitch, and has a quality which may be called booming. *Per contra,* the second sound is shorter, weaker, higher in pitch, and has a quality which may be called valvular or clicking. Aside from the relative length of the two sounds, the other characters are more or less marked in different healthy persons.

These distinctive characters of the heart-sounds are apparent when the ear or stethoscope is applied over the apex. At the base of the heart, that is, in the second intercostal space near the sternum, the characters of the first sound are not the same. The second sound in this situation is louder than the first. This sound is said to be accentuated at the base, the first sound being accentuated at the apex. Moreover, the first sound at the base may not be longer than the second; it loses more or less of its booming quality, the pitch remaining lower than that of the second sound. Removing the ear or the stethoscope a certain distance from the apex in any direction, occasions similar changes in the characters of the first sound. The interposition of several thicknesses of a napkin has the same effect.

From the differential characters over the apex, and the rhythm in other situations, there is no difficulty in distinguishing the first from the second sound in health. In cases of disease, however, owing to disturbance of the rhythm, modifications of the characters of the first sound, and the absence sometimes of one of the sounds, other means of recognition must be resorted to. If the apex-beat can be felt, this offers a ready way for recognizing the first sound—the sound which is synchronous with the apex-beat is, of course, the first sound. This mode is not always available, inasmuch as the apex-beat cannot always be felt. Another mode is always available, namely, feeling the carotid pulse. The carotid pulse is synchronous with the first sound, whereas there is a slight interval between this sound and the radial pulse.

The student is aided in comprehending certain physical signs by taking into view the mechanism of the production of the heart-sounds. The second sound is produced by the sudden forcible closure of the aortic and the pulmonic valve. This closure is caused by a retrograde movement of the columns of blood in the aorta and pulmonary artery, directly the ventricular systole is ended. The retrograde movement is due to the recoil of the coats of the arteries which have been dilated by the column of blood moving onward during the ventricular systole. This recoil causes regurgitation into the ventricle when either the aortic or the pulmonic valve is rendered incompetent by lesions. The mechanism of the first sound is less simple. This sound is in part due to the forcible tension of the auricular-ventricular valves, caused by the systole of the ventricles. In this way is produced a valvular element of the first sound. That the impulsion of heart against the walls of the chest furnishes another element seems demonstrable. To this element of impulsion the first sound is indebted for its greater intensity, as compared with the second sound, its length, and its booming quality. This is shown by the fact, already stated, that when auscultation is made at a certain distance from the apex, these characters are eliminated, and by the fact that diseases which diminish or arrest the impulsion movements of the heart produce the same modifications. The valvular element of the first sound is weaker than the second sound, a fact which at first occasions surprise when the difference in size between the aortic and pulmonic and the auriculo-ventricular valves is considered. The explanation of this apparent incongruity is as follows: the aortic and pulmonic segments at the end of the ventricular systole are in contact with the arterial walls, and are expanded when the recoil of the latter follows. On the other hand, when the ventricular systole takes place in health, the auriculo-ventricular valves are not in contact with the walls of the ventricles, but they are floated out and the orifices are nearly or quite closed; the movement of the blood, therefore, in the systole only renders these valves tense. The second sound, in other words, is due to the expansion of the sigmoid valves of the aorta and pulmonary artery, whereas, the valvular element of the first sound is due to the tension of the auriculo-ventricular valves. The foregoing points relating to the heart-sounds were contained in my prize essay "On the Clinical Study of the Heart-Sounds in Health and Disease," published in the Transactions of the American Medical Association in 1858[7].

A point in relation to the second sound of the heart has an interesting and important bearing on auscultation in disease, namely, the study of this sound as produced at the aortic and the pulmonic orifice separately. Recalling the anatomical relations of the aorta and the pulmonary artery to the walls of the chest, if the stethoscope be applied in the second intercostal space on the right side close to the sternum, the characters of the second sound are derived chiefly from the aortic valve, and if the stethoscope be applied in the second intercostal space on the left side close to the sternum, the characters of the second sound are derived chiefly from the pulmonic valve. The correctness of this statement is proved by differences in the characters of the sound on the two sides in health, and by the modifications in cases of disease. These morbid modifications will enter into the physical diagnosis of cardiac affections. In health the aortic second sound is somewhat louder, higher in pitch, and the valvular quality more marked than the pulmonic second sound. The student should verify these points of difference by the study of the second sound in the two situations just named. In order for the comparison to be a fair one in health and available in the diagnosis of disease, the normal anatomical relations to the walls of the chest, of the aorta, and pulmonary artery must be pre-

---

7 *Vide,* also, "Treatise on Diseases of the Heart," first edition 1860; second edition 1870.

served. These relations are affected by changes in the symmetry of the chest, and sometimes by enlargement of the heart. The lungs must also be free from disease; otherwise, the conduction of the sounds will be abnormal.

The movements of the auricles and the ventricles are to be kept in mind with reference to the understanding of certain physical signs of disease. Points of especial importance are the contraction of the auricles in the latter part of the long pause of the heart, preceding the ventricular systole, and the twisting of the heart from left to right in the systole, this movement being reversed in the diastole. In these systolic and diastolic twisting movements, the pericardial surfaces move upon each, but in health noiselessly owing to their smoothness and moisture. The movements occasion an auscultatory sound when the surfaces are roughened by the presence of lymph. Other points are the size of the pericardial sac, that is, its capability of holding when filled, but not dilated, from fifteen to twenty ounces of liquid, and its attachment, not to the base of the heart, but to the vessels above the base.

Physical Conditions of the Heart in Disease.

The physical conditions of the heart in disease, which are determinable by physical exploration, are, 1st, enlargement of the heart; 2d, abnormal impulses and modifications of the apex-beat; 3rd, valvular lesions; 4th, roughness of the pericardial surfaces; and, 5th, liquid within the pericardial sac. Having considered these conditions, an account of abnormal modifications of the heart-sounds and cardiac murmurs will conclude this chapter.

Enlargement of the Heart.—Enlargement of the heart may be slight, moderate, great, or very great, these terms expressing different degrees of enlargement with sufficient precision for clinical purposes. In cases of very great enlargement, the space within the chest which the heart occupies may be from four to five times larger than in health. The situation of the base of the heart remains but little, or not at all, changed in cases of enlargement; the increased space which the heart occupies is therefore downward. This increased space extends much more to the left than to the right; the left border of the heart, in proportion to the enlargement, is carried beyond the mammary line on the left side, whereas, the right border is carried comparatively but little beyond the normal right lateral boundary of the præcordia even when the enlargement is very great. The superficial cardiac space is enlarged in proportion to the enlargement of the heart; the organ pushes to the left the receding anterior border of the upper lobe of the left lung, and is proportionately in contact, uncovered of lung, with the walls of the chest. The apex of the heart is lowered in proportion to the enlargement, and it is carried more or less to the left of its normal situation. It may be lowered to the sixth, seventh, eighth, or ninth intercostal space. The enlargement of the heart is rarely equal in all its parts. The enlargement may be entirely or chiefly of either the right or the left ventricle. Enlargement of the right ventricle and auricle tends to carry the right side of the heart more to the right than when the left ventricle and auricle are enlarged. The situation of the apex is also affected by the parts of the heart in which the enlargement predominates. The apex is carried further to the left of its normal situation, other things being equal, when the enlargement predominates on the right side of the heart; and it is lowered without being carried far to the left when the enlargement of the left ventricle predominates. The apex of the organ in cases of considerable or of great enlargement becomes changed in form; it is rounded or blunted. This change is moat marked when enlargement of the right ventricle predominates. All these points are of importance with reference to the comprehension of the physical signs of enlargement of the heart.

Enlargement of the heart may be entirely due either to hypertrophy or to dilatation (simple hypertrophy and simple dilatation). If, however, the enlargement be sufficient to occasion notable disturbance of the circulation, both these forms of enlargement are usually combined, but, as a rule, one or the other form predominating, so that, of the cases of disease of the heart which come under medical treatment, the majority are cases of either enlargement with predominant hypertrophy or enlargement with predominant dilatation.

These widely different physical conditions are concerned especially in the abnormal impulses and modifications of the apex-beat, as well as, also, the heart-sounds.

Abnormal Impulses of the Heart, and Modifications of the Apex-beat.—The abnormal situation of the apex of the heart when enlarged has been stated. Generally the situation is determinable by the apex-beat. It has been seen that in health the beat is sometimes not appreciable by the touch, owing to the thickness of the soft parts and the conformation of the thorax, and, for these reasons, the force of the beat varies much in different healthy persons. Exclusive of normal variations, the beat is generally strong and prolonged in proportion as the heart is enlarged by hypertrophy. There are exceptions to this statement, which are to be explained by the altered form of the apex; when it loses its pointed form, it does not so readily come into contact with the walls of the chest in the intercostal space, and, hence, the beat may be weak although the ventricular systole be abnormally powerful. On the other hand, the apex-beat is weakened by dilatation, and it may be wanting as a result of diminished power of the systole of the ventricles. The apex-beat is also abnormally weak in fatty degeneration and softening of the heart, as well as in functional debility of the organ incident to other diseases than those of the heart.

If there be considerable or great enlargement, the heart being in contact with the walls of the chest over a larger area than in health, impulses other than the apex-beat are generally apparent to the eye and touch. Not infrequently impulses are appreciable in each intercostal space between the situation of the apex and the base of the heart. These abnormal impulses are felt to be strong in proportion as the enlargement is due to hypertrophy, and weak in proportion as dilatation predominates. Enlargement seated in the right ventricle causes an impulse in the epigastrium, which is strong or weak in proportion as hypertrophy or dilatation predominates. Cardiac impulses are felt and seen in abnormal situations when the heart is removed from its normal situation by the pressure of an aneurism, or other tumor, by pleuritic effusion, hydroperitoneum, etc. The error of mistaking for a cardiac impulse the pulsation of an aneurismal tumor is to be avoided. Another error is to be avoided, namely, mistaking abnormal impulses due to the heart being uncovered of lung from shrinking of the latter in certain pulmonary affections, for impulses denoting enlargement of the heart. In cases of enlargement by hypertrophy, a heaving movement of the whole præcordia is sometimes felt when the hand is applied to the chest. A violent shock is sometimes felt by the hand applied to the præcordia, but without a sense of increased muscular power, in cases of purely functional disorder of the heart.

Valvular Lesions.—The lesions affecting the valves of the heart are of a varied character, for an account of which the student is referred to treatises on cardiac diseases, or on pathological anatomy. It suffices here to consider that, with reference to physical signs and pathological effects, they may be distributed into three groups, as follows: 1st, lesions which diminish more or less the size of the orifices, or obstructive lesions; 2d, lesions which render the valves more or less incompetent and permit regurgitation, or regurgitative lesions; and, 3d, lesions which roughen the surface over which the blood moves, without occasioning either obstruction or regurgitation. The latter may be distinguished as innocuous lesions, giving rise to no pathological effects, although represented by cardiac murmurs.

It is useful to bear in mind that, in the great majority of cases, valvular lesions are seated in the left side of the heart, that is, they are either mitral or aortic. Tricuspid and pulmonic lesions are comparatively rare, and they are generally congenital. Not infrequently mitral and aortic lesions coexist, and there may be coexisting lesions at all the orifices of the heart.

Valvular lesions are represented by cardiac murmurs. By means of the murmurs the existence of lesions is evidenced, their situation at the different orifices may be ascertained, and, generally, it is practicable to determine whether they occasion obstruction or regurgitation, or both. These several points of inquiry will be considered presently under the heading cardiac murmurs, and in connection with the lesions of the different valves respectively in the next chapter.

Roughness of the Pericardial Surfaces.—In place of the smoothness of the pericardial surfaces in health, which permits their movements upon each other noiselessly, the presence of the inflammatory product lymph, and, in some rare instances morbid growths, occasion an adventitious sound or murmur, which will be noticed in connection with other murmurs, and as entering into the physical diagnosis of pericarditis.

Liquid within the Pericardial Sac.—More or less liquid transudes into the pericardial sac in cases of general dropsy or anasarca, but rarely in very large quantity. Liquid effusion occurs in acute pericarditis, and in this affection the sac may become filled with liquid. In some cases of chronic pericarditis the sac is greatly dilated by liquid, the quantity amounting to four pounds, or even more.

When the pericardial sac is filled with liquid, without being dilated, it forms, virtually, a pyriform tumor within the chest, the base of which is at the sixth or seventh intercostal space; the apex rises nearly to the sternal notch; the left lateral border is considerably beyond the nipple, and the right lateral border is more or less beyond the right margin of the præcordia. The anterior portion of the filled pericardium is mostly uncovered of lung and in contact with the walls of the chest. Within this area there is either notable dulness or flatness on percussion, together with absence of respiratory murmur and of vocal resonance. By means of these signs, the boundaries of the pyriform tumor may be readily delineated on the surface of the chest.

When the pericardial sac is partially filled with liquid, the same signs are present, but within an area of less extent, and the configuration of the pyriform tumor is wanting.

In cases of chronic pericarditis with a large accumulation of liquid, the pericardial sac is dilated so that its lateral boundaries may extend nearly to the axillary and infra-axillary regions. Under these circumstances, flatness on percussion, absence of respiratory murmur and of vocal resonance, are present over the greater part of the anterior aspect of the chest.

Abnormal Modifications of the Heart-sounds.

In order to appreciate the abnormal modifications of the heart-sounds, their normal characters are to be kept in mind (***vide*** page 195), and the student must be practically familiar with them. The modifications relate especially to the intensity and quality of the first and the second sound. Either of the two sounds may be suppressed.

The first sound has all its normal characters intensified when the power of the ventricular systole is increased by hypertrophy. The sound is louder than in health; it is longer, and the booming quality is more marked. If obstructive or regurgitant valvular lesions do not exist, the second sound is also intensified, without change in other respects. The first sound, when much intensified, sometimes has a ringing tone or tinnitus. This is also sometimes observed in health when the power of the heart's action from any cause is increased.

In some cases of violent palpitation the first sound is notably intense, but short and valvular in quality. I suppose the explanation of this to be as follows: the ventricles contract with a kind of spasmodic action upon a small quantity of blood; and, under these circumstances, the auriculo-ventricular valves, not being floated out as they are when the ventricles are well filled, expand with force in the ventricular systole, instead of being merely made tense as in health. Hence, the valvular element of the first sound is much intensified, while those characters of the first sound which are due to the impulsion of the heart against the walls of the chest, may be feeble or wanting.

Weakening or suppression of the first sound over the apex is an effect of those affections of the heart which diminish the power of the ventricular systole. These affections are enlargement from dilatation, atrophy, fatty degeneration, and softening. If the sound be notably weakened, it becomes short and valvular like the second sound. These changes show that the characters dependent on the element of impulsion are affected more than the valvular element. Liquid effusion within the pericardium renders the first sound more or leas weak and valvular, the characters derived from impulsion being, under these circumstances, wanting. Diminished power of the heart's action from other than cardiac diseases, involves weakness of both of the heart-sounds, but more especially of the first sound.

The abnormal modifications of the second sound, which are chiefly of interest and importance, relate to the aortic and pulmonic sound considered separately. Bearing in mind the mode of interrogating the aortic and the pulmonic orifice with reference to the valvular sound derived from each independently of the other (***vide*** page 199), a comparison of the two sounds in diseases of the heart affords often useful information. Whenever, from mitral obstruction or regurgitant lesions, or both combined, the blood propelled by the left ventricle into the aorta is diminished, the recoil of the arterial coats, after the ventricular systole, is lessened; consequently, the aortic segments expand with less force, and the valvular sound is weakened. Diminished intensity of the aortic sound thus represents an abnormal diminution of the quantity of blood propelled into the systemic arteries in the systole of the left ventricle, and this diminished intensity is, in a measure, a criterion of the amount of mitral obstruction or mitral regurgitation, or both combined. In some cases of extreme obstruction or regurgitation, the aortic sound is completely suppressed. How is weakening of this sound to be determined and measured? By comparison with the pulmonic sound. Now, as will presently appear, the pulmonic sound is apt to be intensified when the aortic sound is weakened. Hence, the former is not an accurate standard for this comparison; but it suffices for an approximation to accuracy. In cases of hypertrophy of the left ventricle without obstructive or regurgitant valvular lesions, the aortic sound is abnormally intensified. These cases are, however, of rare occurrence. They occur chiefly in connection with fibroid or atrophic lesions of the kidneys.

A simpler cause of weakening or suppression of the aortic sound, is damage from lesions of the aortic valve. In proportion as the function of this valve is impaired by lesions, the intensity of the sound is diminished, and if the function of the valve be lost, the sound is wanting. In these cases, the pulmonic sound being but little or not at all affected, it is an accurate standard for the comparison.

The pulmonic sound is weakened in the rare instances of lesions affecting the pulmonic valve. This sound is oftener intensified than weakened. It is notably intensified when the right ventricle is hypertrophied, and especially when this hypertrophy is associated with dilatation of the left auricle resulting from mitral obstruction or regurgitation. These lesions weakening, as has just been seen, the aortic sound, the contrast between the aortic and the pulmonic sound in some cases of mitral lesions is very marked. The pulmonic sound is sometimes loud while the aortic sound is suppressed.

In comparing the aortic and the pulmonic sound in disease, as in health, it is to be assumed that the anatomical relations of the aortic and the pulmonary artery to the second intercostal space on either side, close to the sternum, are not materially altered, and that the lungs are free from lesions in consequence of which the conduction of the sound on either side is abnormal.

Returning to the first sound of the heart, the mitral and the tricuspid part of the valvular element of this sound may be studied separately. With the stethoscope applied at or a little to the left of the apex, the valvular element of the first sound, which is heard, is derived chiefly from the mitral valve. On the other hand, if the stethoscope be applied at or near the right lower border of the heart, the valvular element is derived chiefly from the tricuspid valve. Notable weakness or suppression of the mitral valvular sound as compared with the tricuspid, represents impairment of the function of the mitral valve, and, per contra, notable weakness or suppression of the tricuspid valvular sound denotes impairment of the function of the tricuspid valve. Allowance, in this comparison, is to be made for a normal disparity, the mitral valvular sound being louder than the tricuspid, in health.

Reduplication of Heart-sounds.—The sounds of the heart are said to be reduplicated when either the first or the second sound is repeated, or when each sound occurs twice before the long pause or interval. Considering the heart-sounds as represented by the whispered words Lub-dup, reduplication of the first sound is expressed by Lub lub-dup, of the second by Lub-dup dup, and of both sounds by Lub lub-dup dup.

Clinically, reduplication of the second sound is much more frequent than reduplication of either the first sound, or of both sounds. Yet, accepting the explanation which seems most reasonable of this anomaly, both sounds should always be reduplicated, that is, neither should be reduplicated separately. It is probable that both sounds are always reduplicated, but the reduplication of one of them (generally the first sound) from its feebleness is not appreciable.

There is a form of disorder which may be confounded with reduplication of both sounds of the heart. In this disorder, with every alternate revolution of the heart, the sounds are weak, and the ventricular systole is not represented by a radial pulse, the force of the contraction of the ventricle being insufficient to cause an appreciable pulsation in the remote arteries; hence, the heart-sounds occur twice for each pulse at the wrist. Under these circumstances, however, the carotid pulse may generally, if not always, be felt with the weak, as well as with the stronger, ventricular contraction, and in this way the error of confounding the disorder with reduplication may be avoided.

The explanation of reduplication is, that instead of the two ventricles contracting in unison, as in health, one contracts a little before the other. This explanation accounts satisfactorily for the anomaly.

Reduplication of the heart-sounds may occur in connection with cardiac lesions, or there may be no evidence of any organic affection. In the latter case, the anomaly falls properly among the varied forms of functional disorder of the heart. Whether or not it be connected with lesions, it has no important pathological significance. It is usually of temporary duration.

Cardiac Murmurs.

All adventitious, abnormal sounds which are added to the heart-sounds, are embraced by the term cardiac murmurs. Let it be borne in mind that, conventionally, the murmurs are never abnormal modifications of the heart-sounds, but always newly produced sounds, and they always represent morbid conditions of either the heart or the blood. When due to morbid conditions of the blood, they are called inorganic, anæmic, hæmic murmurs, and when they represent valvular lesions or changes within the heart, they are distinguished as organic murmurs.

The organic murmurs may be distributed into three groups after differences in quality, namely, 1st, soft; 2d, rough; and 3d, musical murmurs. The soft murmurs resemble the sound produced by air from the nozzle of a pair of bellows, and, hence, are often called bellows murmurs. Murmurs are said to be rough when their qualities may be expressed by such terms as rasping, grating, creaking, croaking, etc. They are called musical when the sound is a musical note. The bellows murmurs are of most frequent occurrence, and the musical are much more rare than the rough murmurs. The quality of a murmur does not in general invest it with any special pathological or diagnostic significance. The murmurs vary in pitch, being either relatively high or low. The variations in pitch are useful in aiding to discriminate different coexisting murmurs.

This account of organic murmurs applies to those produced at the orifices or within the cavities of the heart. They are distinguished as endocardial murmurs. Adventitious sounds are, however, produced upon the external surface of the heart. These constitute what is called exocardial, pericardial, or friction murmur.

Endocardial murmurs are produced by blood-currents pursuing either a normal or an abnormal direction. With a familiar knowledge of these currents, and of their relations with the heart-sounds, the several endocardial murmurs are very easily understood, as regards points involved in their differentiation from each other. The student is, therefore, advised first to become acquainted with the blood-currents, in health and in disease. Directing the attention to the left side of the heart, there are two normal blood-currents, namely, the current from the left auricle to the left ventricle, and the current from the left ventricle into the aorta. These may be distinguished as the direct currents. The first is the mitral direct current, and the second is the aortic direct current. Two abnormal currents may occur in the left side of the heart. These currents can only take place when the valves are rendered incompetent by lesions. The incompetency of the valves allows of regurgitation, and these abnormal currents may be distinguished as the regurgitant currents. One of these is a current backward from the left ventricle into the left auricle, owing to incompetency of the mitral valve; this is the mitral regurgitant current. The other is a current backward from the aorta into the left ventricle, arising from incompetency of the aortic valve; this is the aortic regurgitant current.

What are the relations of these four currents in the left side of the heart with the heart-sounds? The mitral direct current takes place when the auricles contract. The contraction of the auricles precedes the ventricular systole. The ventricular systole is synchronous with the first sound of the heart. The mitral direct current, therefore, takes place just before the first sound of the heart. It begins after the second sound, and continues until it is suddenly and completely arrested by the contraction of the ventricle. It is obvious that the current cannot continue during the ventricular contraction, that is, when the first sound of the heart is produced. The mitral regurgitant current is caused by the contraction of the ventricle; the current, therefore, must take place with the first sound of the heart. This current is systolic in the time of its occurrence. The aortic direct current, being caused by the contraction of the left ventricle, takes place with the first sound of the heart. It is, therefore, coincident with the mitral regurgitant current. The aortic regurgitant current is caused by the recoil of the arterial coats upon the column of blood within the aorta directly after the ventricular systole, and as this recoil causes the second sound of the heart, the current and this sound must be coincident.

Recapitulating the relations of the four currents with the heart-sounds, the aortic direct and the mitral regurgitant take place with the first sound—they are systolic currents; the mitral direct current precedes the first sound—it is presystolic, and the aortic regurgitant current takes place with the second sound—it is diastolic.

Analogous blood-currents take place in the right side of the heart, and have corresponding relations with the heart-sounds. These currents are the tricuspid direct, the tricuspid regurgitant, the pulmonic direct, and the pulmonic regurgitant. The pulmonic regurgitant is exceedingly rare in consequence of the infrequency of pulmonic lesions; but the tricuspid regurgitant is not uncommon, and probably occurs without valvular lesions or enlargement of the heart the right ventricle is distended with blood, constituting what has been called the "safety valve function" of the tricuspid orifice.

Organic endocardial murmurs are produced by the foregoing direct and regurgitant blood currents, and they are designated by the same names, that is, they are either direct or regurgitant. Thus, there are produced in the left side of the heart—

the side in which vulvular lesions are seated in the great majority of cases—a mitral direct murmur, a mitral regurgitant murmur, an aortic direct murmur, and an aortic regurgitant murmur. In the right side of the heart there may be produced corresponding murmurs, namely, a tricuspid direct, a tricuspid regurgitant, a pulmonic direct, and a pulmonic regurgitant. It remains to point out the means of differentiating these several murmurs aside from their relations with the heart-sounds.

Mitral Direct Murmur.—This murmur is presystolic. It begins after the second sound and ends abruptly with the first sound. Almost invariably this murmur is rough in quality; occasionally it is a soft bellows murmur. When rough it is often quite loud. The rough quality is peculiar; it is suggestive of vibration, and may be imitated by causing the lips or the tongue to vibrate with the breath in expiration. I state the mechanism of this murmur, inasmuch as the explanation is original with me, and has not been as yet generally accepted. It is caused by the vibration of the mitral curtains, and takes place especially when these curtains are united at their sides, leaving a narrowed orifice through which the mitral direct current of blood flows. Throwing the lips into vibration with the breath, represents not only the quality of the murmur, but the mode of its production. The physical conditions which are requisite generally for its production are a narrowed mitral orifice, and flaccidity of the mitral curtains. The latter of these conditions does not always exist in cases of mitral obstructive lesions, and, hence, the murmur by no means always accompanies these lesions. When it is considered how loud a blubbering sound may be produced by the vibration of the lips with a feeble current of air, it is not difficult to understand that an intense murmur may be caused by a current of blood propelled by the comparatively weak contraction of the auricle.

A mitral direct murmur may be produced without mitral lesions, the murmur having the same rough quality as when lesions exist, and being also quite loud. This statement, based on clinical proof, was made by me many years since, together with the explanation. It occurs when there are aortic lesions which permit free regurgitation. Under these circumstances, at the time when the auricular contraction takes place, the left ventricle is already filled with blood; the mitral curtains are floated out so as to be in contact with each other, and the mitral direct current passing between the curtains throws them into vibration precisely as when the orifice is narrowed. The vibration of the lips when lightly in contact, caused by the expired breath, illustrates the manner in which a mitral direct murmur takes place without mitral lesions. The murmur, thus occurring without mitral lesions, is not constant; it is now present and now absent, depending, as it does, on the quantity of blood within the left ventricle at the time of the contraction of the auricle. It follows from what has just been stated, that a mitral direct murmur is not always a sign of mitral obstructive lesions, when there is free aortic regurgitation.

This murmur is limited to a circumscribed space around the apex of the heart. However loud the murmur may be in this situation, it is lost within a short distance from the apex.

A mitral direct murmur is never due to a morbid condition of the blood. Although it occurs without mitral lesions, yet, inasmuch as its occurrence then requires the existence of aortic regurgitant lesions, it cannot be said to be an inorganic murmur.

Mitral Regurgitant Murmur; Mitral Systolic Non-regurgitant, or Intraventricular Murmur.—The mitral regurgitant murmur, synchronous with the first sound, that is, a systolic murmur, may be soft, rough, or musical in quality, its intensity and pitch being variable. Aside from its relation with the first sound of the heart, it is distinguished by having its maximum of intensity at or near the situation of the apex-beat. It may be limited to a circumscribed area, and if heard at a distance from the apex, it is best transmitted laterally around the left side of the chest. It is often heard on the posterior aspect of the chest on the left side near the lower angle of the scapula, and not infrequently in the corresponding situation on the right side.

A murmur with the first sound heard within a limited area at the apex, may be due to roughness of the endocardial membrane without mitral incompetency, and, consequently, without a mitral regurgitant current. This is a mitral systolic non-regurgitant murmur. It may also be called an intra-ventricular murmur, being produced, not at the mitral orifice, but within the ventricle. This murmur cannot always be discriminated from a feeble mitral regurgitant murmur. If, however, a mitral murmur be conducted laterally for some distance to the left of the apex, and if it be heard on the back, it may be considered to represent mitral regurgitation. A mitral systolic, non-regurgitant, or intra-ventricular murmur, is the murmur present in endocarditis.

It is probable that the impulse of the apex of the heart against the adjacent portion of lung sometimes forces the air from the air vesicles sufficiently to give rise to a blowing sound occurring with each ventricular systole. This is liable to be confounded with an endocardial murmur. Produced in the way just stated, it may be heard only during the act of inspiration, and especially at the end of this act.

A mitral systolic murmur is rarely, if ever, due to an abnormal condition of the blood, without any anatomical change in the valve or endocardial membrane. Conditions of the blood, however, which are favorable for the production of inorganic murmurs, may intensify this murmur as well as any of the organic murmurs.

Aortic. Direct Murmur.—This murmur, like the mitral regurgitant, and the mitral systolic non-regurgitant murmur, occurs with the first sound of the heart, that is, it is systolic. Of the organic murmurs in the left side of the heart, the murmurs just named and the aortic direct murmur, are synchronous, the others having different relations with the heart-sounds. The aortic direct murmur differs from the mitral systolic murmur in having its maximum of intensity at the base of the heart. It is loudest in the second intercostal space near the sternum. As a rule, it is louder in this intercostal space on the right than on the left side; this rule, however, has frequent exceptions. It is transmitted better and further upward than downward. It is always heard over the carotid artery; and it is sometimes louder over this artery than at the base of the heart. As a murmur may be produced within the carotid artery, it is desirable to determine, when a systolic murmur is heard at the base, whether the carotid murmur is a transmitted murmur or not. This point is to be settled by comparing the murmur over the carotid with the murmur at the base, as regards quality and pitch. If the quality and pitch of the murmur in the two situations are the same, it is fair to consider the murmur in the carotid as not produced within the artery, but conducted by the blood current from the aortic orifice.

An aortic direct murmur is frequently inorganic. It is to be considered as such when it is not associated with an aortic regurgitant murmur; when the heart is not enlarged; when anæmia is shown by the presence of murmurs in the large arteries; and when there is the venous hum in the neck—these physical evidences of anæmia being associated with pallor or with symptoms pointing to that condition of the blood. Moreover, an inorganic murmur is very rarely rough, and it is variable in its occurrence, being at one time present and at another time absent, whereas, an organic murmur is, in general, constant. Associated with other evidence of anæmia, an aortic direct murmur may, nevertheless, be organic, but, under the differentiating circumstances just stated, the lesion represented by the murmur, if the murmur be organic, must be innocuous, so that it is not of great practical importance to determine whether the murmur be or be not inorganic.

Like the other organic murmurs, an aortic direct murmur varies in different cases in its intensity, quality, and pitch. An organic aortic direct murmur, ***per se,*** does not denote always aortic obstruction. It may be due simply to roughness of the membrane at or above the aortic orifice.

Aortic Regurgitant Murmur; Aortic Diastolic Non-regurgitant Murmur.—An aortic regurgitant murmur occurs with the second sound of the heart, and it is the only one of the organic murmurs produced in the left side of the heart which has this relation with the heart-sounds. It is, therefore, readily enough discriminated from the other murmurs. It is almost always heard at the base of the heart, but, in some instances, when not appreciable at the base, it is heard a little below the base, namely, near the sternum on the left side on a level with the fourth costal cartilage. In the latter situation it has generally its maximum of intensity. It is transmitted best in a downward direction, being often heard at the apex, and sometimes considerably below this point. It is never inorganic. It is usually not intense, low in pitch and soft; but it may be loud, high, rough, or musical.

A short murmur is sometimes produced by the retrograde movement of the blood-current within the aorta, the aortic valve being sufficient, and regurgitation not therefore taking place. This murmur is due to roughening of the lining membrane of the aorta by atheroma or calcareous deposit, and it, is always preceded by an aortic direct murmur. It occurs directly after the systole, and ends with the second sound. Although of such brief duration, it is distinctly recognizable and distinguished from the preceding aortic direct murmur. I have long been accustomed to demonstrate this murmur in private teaching, and have called it an aortic diastolic non-regurgitant murmur. It cannot be said to have practical importance, inasmuch as the lesion giving rise to it is represented by the aortic direct murmur which precedes it.

Coexisting Endocardial Murmurs.—The murmurs referable to the left side of the heart, which have been considered, are often found in combination; two or three may coexist, or all of them may be present. Moreover, with more or less of these murmurs may be associated murmurs referable to the right side of the heart.

Having become familiar with their relations with the heart-sounds, and other points involved in their differentiation, it is not difficult to recognize them in combination. The mitral murmurs are not infrequently associated. The mitral direct, being presystolic, ends with the first sound, and the mitral systolic or regurgitant begins with this sound; the first sound, as it were, divides these two murmurs. The murmurs almost invariably differ from each other in pitch and quality. The presence of both, in fact, assists, rather than obstructs, the recognition of each. The aortic direct and the aortic regurgitant murmur, also, are often associated. A murmur then accompanies the first and the second sound of the heart; the two murmurs follow in the same rhythmical order as the heart-sounds. These murmurs, when associated, can only be confounded with pericardial friction sounds.

The combination of the aortic direct and the mitral systolic murmur alone offers any difficulty. These two murmurs have the same relation with the heart-sounds; they are both systolic. How is it to be determined, when a systolic murmur is heard both at the base and apex, that either a mitral murmur is transmitted to the base, or an aortic murmur is transmitted to the apex; in other words, how is it to be decided whether two murmurs are present or only one murmur? If these two murmurs coexist, generally the circumstances which distinguish each separately can be ascertained. Thus, the aortic murmur is transmitted into the carotid artery, and the presence of that murmur is then established; the mitral regurgitant murmur is often transmitted laterally around the chest or heard at the lower angle of the scapula, and then the presence of that murmur is established. But there are additional points, namely, the murmur at the base and that at the apex generally differ sufficiently in pitch or quality to render it evident that there are two murmurs; and generally at a situation in the præcordia between the base and apex, both murmurs may be either lost or become notably weakened. Attention to these points in most instances divests the problem of difficulty.

Mitral and aortic lesions are often of a character to give rise to only one murmur at either of these orifices. A mitral direct murmur not infrequently is present without the mitral regurgitant, and the reverse of this is frequent. So either an aortic direct or an aortic regurgitant murmur may exist without the other.

Tricuspid Direct Murmur.—The lesions which are requisite for this murmur very rarely occur at the tricuspid orifice; hence, this murmur is exceedingly rare. It is to be distinguished from the mitral direct murmur by its localization being, not at the apex, but at the right border of the heart. The mitral direct and the tricuspid direct murmur may coexist; an instance of this kind has fallen under my observation. In that instance a presystolic murmur, with the characteristic blubbering quality, was heard both at the apex and at the right side of the heart.

Tricuspid Regurgitant Murmur.—This murmur is not of very infrequent occurrence. Tricuspid regurgitation occurs often when the right ventricle is considerably dilated, without the existence of lesions of the valve. A tricuspid regurgitation current, however, does not invariably give rise to an appreciable murmur. This fact is shown by the occurrence of a venous pulse in the neck, due to tricuspid regurgitation, when no murmur can be heard.

The tricuspid regurgitant murmur, of course, occurs with the first sound, being systolic like the mitral regurgitant murmur, and the latter generally coexists. It is distinguished from the mitral regurgitant by its localization at the right inferior margin of the heart, and its transmission to the right rather than to the left. The coexistence of the mitral and the tricuspid regurgitant murmur is determined by the differences in pitch and quality between a systolic murmur at the apex and at the right margin of the heart. A venous pulse synchronous with the first sound of the heart, points to tricuspid regurgitation, and, although sometimes present without a tricuspid regurgitant murmur, when present it is corroborative evidence of the latter.

Pulmonic Direct Murmur.—A pulmonic direct murmur, if organic, is generally connected with congenital lesions. The pulmonic direct and the aortic direct current of blood taking place at the same instant, the murmurs representing both are, of course, systolic. How is the pulmonic to be distinguished from the aortic direct murmur? The pulmonic murmur is heard in the left second intercostal space close to the sternum; but this is not very distinctive, inasmuch as, not infrequently, the aortic murmur is loudest in that situation. The essential point of distinction is this: the pulmonic direct murmur is not transmitted into the carotid artery, whereas, the aortic direct murmur is always thus transmitted. If an aortic direct and a pulmonic direct murmur coexist, both being organic, the combination is to be ascertained by finding that the murmur in the second intercostal space on the right side differs from that on the left side in pitch or quality, sufficiently to show the presence of two murmurs, the one on the right side being transmitted to the carotid artery.

An inorganic pulmonic direct murmur is of frequent occurrence. It is generally associated with an inorganic aortic direct murmur, the presence of the two murmurs being evidenced by a difference in pitch.

Pulmonic Regurgitant Murmur.—This murmur must be exceedingly rare. It occurs, of course, like the aortic regurgitant, with the second sound. Its presence can only be determined when other signs go to show the existence of pulmonic and the absence of aortic lesions. This murmur, as well as the aortic regurgitant, can never be inorganic, its presence being proof of a regurgitant current of blood from incompetency of the pulmonic valve.

Facts of practical importance in relation to the endocardial murmurs, are embraced in the following statements:—

The question as to a murmur being organic or inorganic, relates chiefly, if not entirely, to the aortic direct and the pulmonic direct murmur, other murmurs being almost invariably, if not invariably, organic.

Associated signs and symptoms generally warrant a definite conclusion whether an aortic direct or a pulmonic direct murmur be, or be not, organic, and under the circumstances which render it difficult to decide this question positively, a positive decision is not of much immediate practical consequence.

Valvular lesions, whether obstructive, regurgitant, or innocuous, are so uniformly represented by murmur, that, as a rule, absence of lesions may be predicated on the absence of murmur.

With a practical knowledge of the different organic murmurs, the situation of lesions at either of the orifices of the heart, or their existence at two or more of these orifices, may be demonstratively determined.

By means of the murmurs, with other signs, it may be determined demonstratively whether the lesions involve obstruction or regurgitation, or both, or, on the other hand, that they are, as regards immediate pathological effects, innocuous.

The murmurs do not afford definite information as to the amount of obstruction or regurgitation, in other words, as to the pathological importance or gravity of lesions when they are not innocuous. No positive conclusions on this point of view

Pericardial or Friction Murmur.—A pericardial or friction murmur is produced by the rubbing together of the surfaces of the pericardium in the systolic and diastolic movements of the heart. In the vast majority of the cases in which this murmur occurs, it denotes either the presence of recent lymph which renders the surfaces more or less adhesive, or roughening from lymph which has become dense and adherent; its diagnostic significance, therefore, relates almost exclusively to pericarditis. In this relation it is of great practical importance.

This murmur is to be discriminated from the endocardial murmurs. The points involved in the discrimination are as follows: The murmur is double, that is, a murmur accompanies both the ventricular systole and diastole. It can, therefore, only be confounded with an aortic direct and an aortic regurgitant murmur in combination. The quality of the murmur is suggestive of rubbing or friction. It is sometimes a feeble, grazing sound; in other instances it is loud and quite rough. When rough, the quality is expressed by such terms as rasping, grating, creaking, etc. Although accompanying both sounds of the heart, it has not that uniform, fixed relation to these sounds which characterizes the aortic direct and the aortic regurgitant murmur; it is not in definite accord with the heart-sounds. Moreover, in intensity it varies with the successive movements of the heart, being louder with some revolutions than with others, in this regard differing notably from the endocardial murmurs. It is not heard without the præcordia, as a rule, and is often limited to a part of the præcordial region, whereas, certain of the endocardial murmurs, namely, the mitral regurgitant and the aortic direct, are often heard at a considerable distance from the heart. Firm pressure with the stethoscope intensifies the murmur. Its source seems very near the surface of the chest. In this respect it differs notably from endocardial murmurs, the latter appearing to come from a certain distance within the chest. This point of distinction is very appreciable, especially if, as often happens, a friction murmur be associated with an endocardial murmur.

CHAPTER VIII.
THE PHYSICAL DIAGNOSIS OF DISEASES OF THE HEART AND OF THORACIC ANEURISM.

> Enlargement of the heart by hypertrophy and dilatation—Valvular lesions, mitral, aortic, tricuspid, and pulmonic—Fatty degeneration and softening of the heart—Endocarditis—Pericarditis—Functional disorders—Thoracic aneurism.

THE morbid physical conditions incident to the different diseases of the heart, and the signs representing these conditions, have been considered in the preceding chapter. The diseases are now to be considered with reference to the assemblage of signs on which the physical diagnosis of each is to be based. Most of the diseases of the heart may be diagnosticated by means of physical signs. A few cardiac lesions do not admit of a physical diagnosis, and they do not, therefore, claim consideration in this work. The following are the affections which will form separate headings in this chapter: Enlargement of the Heart by Hypertrophy and by Dilatation, Valvular Lesions, Fatty Degeneration and Softening of the Heart, Endocarditis, Pericarditis, and Functional Disorders. Having considered these affections, the physical diagnosis of thoracic aneurism will be the concluding topic.

Enlargement of the Heart by Hypertrophy and by Dilatation.—Physical exploration to determine the size of the heart, has three objects, namely, to determine, first, that the size of the heart is normal; second, that the heart is enlarged; and third, the degree of enlargement. These objects are attainable by means of percussion and auscultation.

The heart is of normal size when the apex-beat is in its normal situation, that is, in the fifth intercostal space, a little within a vertical line passing through the nipple (the linea mammalis); when the superficial cardiac space is not enlarged, as shown by percussion and by auscultation of the voice (*vide* page 194) and when percussion shows the lateral borders of the heart to be situated normally, namely, on the left side a little within the line of the nipple, and on the right side a finger's breadth to the right of the right margin of the sternum. These points of evidence warrant a positive conclusion that the heart is not enlarged.

The fact of an enlargement and its degree are determinable by an abnormal situation of the apex, together with an increase of the superficial cardiac space and extension of the lateral boundaries of the deep cardiac space especially on the left side.

In cases of slight or very moderate enlargement, the apex is situated a little without the linea mammalis, but not below the fifth intercostal space. A somewhat greater enlargement lowers the apex to the sixth intercostal space, and removes it further without the line of the nipple. In greater degrees of enlargement the apex is lowered to the seventh, eighth, or ninth intercostal space, and generally further removed to the left. The lowering of the apex and the removal to the left, are not uniformly proportionate to each other. As a rule, if the right side of the heart be more enlarged than the left, the apex is removed without the linea mammalis further than when the enlargement of the left side of the heart predominates; and when the latter is the case, the apex is lowered out of proportion to its removal without that line. The relatively abnormal situation downward and to the left, thus, is evidence of the enlargement predominating in either the right or the left side of the heart. Generally the situation of the apex is apparent to the touch and frequently to the eye. In some instances, however, the impulse can neither be seen nor felt. How is its situation to be then ascertained? Auscultation furnishes a ready and reliable mode of determining this point. With the stethoscope the situation in which the first sound of the heart has its maximum of intensity, corresponds to the situation of the apex. This is hardly less definite than the presence of an appreciable impulse.

In determining the fact of enlargement and its degree by the abnormal situation of the apex, causes of the latter which are extrinsic to the heart are to be eliminated. The apex is removed to the left of its normal situation by enlargement of the left lobe of the liver, abdominal tumors, hydroperitoneum, the pregnant uterus, and gastric tympanites. These extrinsic conditions are to be excluded or due allowance made for them. In some cases in which one or more of these extrinsic causes of displacement exist, the apex is carried into the axillary region. It is to be borne in mind that these causes of displacement may exist when there is more or less enlargement of the heart. All these causes, while they displace the apex to the left, do not lower, but tend to raise it above its normal situation. On the other hand, an aneurismal or other tumor situated above the heart may press downward the organ, and in this way the apex is more or less lowered.

The superficial cardiac space is increased in proportion as the heart is enlarged. The extent of this increase is easily determined by percussion and auscultation. Within this space there is notable dullness on percussion. The degree of dulness is greater than within the superficial cardiac space in health, and this degree of dulness is proportionate to the greater area in which the heart is uncovered of lung. It is sufficiently easy to delineate by percussion on the chest the boundary of the anterior border of the upper lobe of the left lung, in other words, of the oblique line which is the hypothenuse of the right-angled triangle representing the superficial cardiac space in health and in disease. The area of the superficial cardiac space is also not less readily and precisely ascertained by auscultation of the voice; the limits of the lung within the præcordia are denoted by an abrupt cessation or notable diminution of the vocal resonance. In females, with large mammæ, auscultation is more available for this object than percussion. The extent to which the superficial cardiac space is enlarged is a good criterion of the degree of the enlargement of the heart.

In proportion as the heart is enlarged, the situation of the left border is without the linea mammalis. Its situation is determined by percussion. Dulness, although not great, is sufficiently distinct within the deep cardiac space, and the line which denotes the left border of the heart is easily delineated on the chest. This statement holds true with respect to the right border of the heart; but this border, even when the enlargement of the heart is great, is removed comparatively little to the right of its normal situation. By means of percussion the boundaries of the præcordia as enlarged by the increased size of the heart, may be determined and measured. In making this statement it is assumed that the lungs are not diseased, and that the chest is not deformed. Shrinkage of the upper lobe of the left lung may enlarge the superficial cardiac space, and cause displacement of the heart. The latter is an effect of the presence of pleuritic effusion, and it may follow its removal. In cases of deformity from spinal curvature, to determine the fact of enlargement of the heart, or its degree, is not always an easy problem.

There is a liability to error in localizing the apex in some cases of enlargement. Owing to the blunted form of the apex, especially when the enlargement is chiefly of the right side of the heart, the apex-beat may be quite feeble. It is liable to be overlooked, and a stronger impulse in the intercostal space above the apex, mistaken for the apex-beat. Of course the lowest impulse is the apex-beat. Careful palpation, and finding by auscultation the spot where the first sound has its maximum of intensity, will prevent this error.

Enlargement of the heart, and the degree of enlargement having been ascertained, it is to be determined whether hypertrophy or dilatation predominate. If the enlargement be slight or moderate, it may be a question whether hypertrophy or dilatation exist alone. As a rule, if either of these two forms of enlargement exist without the other, it is hypertrophy, for, with rare exceptions, hypertrophy precedes dilatation. If the enlargement be very great, as a rule, dilatation predominates, for, the capability of hypertrophic increase of size has its limit, and an increase of size beyond this limit must be due to dilatation. The signs denoting, on the one hand, hypertrophy, and, on the other hand, dilatation, relate to the impulses of the heart and to the heart-sounds.

With a moderate enlargement, hypertrophy is to be inferred from an abnormal force of the apex-beat, and an intensification of the characters of the first sound over the apex. With a considerable or great enlargement, if hypertrophy predominate, the apex-beat may be abnormally strong and prolonged, but, as already stated, owing to its blunted form, the beat is sometimes weak and scarcely appreciable. The increased power of the ventricular contractions, representing the hypertrophy, is then to be determined by impulses in the intercostal spaces above the apex. These impulses are sometimes present in each intercostal space between the apex and the base; and they are abnormally strong in proportion as hypertrophy predominates. Still more marked evidence of hypertrophy is sometimes obtained when the hand is placed over the præcordia; a powerful heaving movement is felt. The increased power of the ventricular contractions may in some cases be in this way appreciated somewhat as if the heart were held in the hand. In cases of considerable or great enlargement, the intensity of the first sound, over the apex, is more or less increased; it is prolonged and its booming quality is more marked than in health. Not infrequently it is accompanied by a metallic ringing sound, or tinnitus.

Moderate enlargement by dilatation is characterized by abnormal weakness of the apex-beat, and of the first sound over the apex. Cases, however, of simple dilatation are rare. If the enlargement be considerable or great, and dilatation predominate, all the impulses are weak, as compared with the cases in which hypertrophy predominates, and the first sound over the apex is more or less divested of the characters derived from impulsion; that is, the sound is feeble, short, and valvular. These points of distinction are marked in proportion as dilatation preponderates.

In the great majority of the cases of enlargement of the heart, valvular lesions coexist. These coexisting valvular lesions are represented by endocardial murmurs, and they are excluded by the absence of the latter. In most of the cases in which enlargement exists without valvular lesions, it is associated with either pulmonary emphysema or chronic Bright's disease.

Valvular Lesions.

The physical diagnosis of valvular lesions embraces their localization at the different orifices within the heart, and determining their character as giving rise to obstruction and regurgitation, or their innocuousness in these respects. These objects of diagnosis involve the endocardial murmurs, and the abnormal modifications of the heart-sounds which were considered in the preceding chapter. Lesions at the different orifices, namely, the mitral, aortic, tricuspid, and pulmonic, will be considered separately.

Mitral Lesions.—The lesions at the mitral orifice are represented by the mitral murmurs—the mitral direct murmur, the mitral regurgitant, and the mitral systolic non-regurgitant or intra-ventricular murmur. Mitral obstructive lesions exist whenever the mitral direct murmur is present, with an exception already stated and explained (*vide* p. 216), namely, this murmur is present in some cases in which the mitral valve is intact, aortic lesions, giving rise to free regurgitation, existing in these cases. These exceptional instances are rare, and I am not aware that any have been reported except by myself.

Mitral regurgitant lesions exist whenever a mitral murmur which is truly regurgitant is present. A systolic murmur having its maximum of intensity at or near the apex, transmitted laterally for a certain distance beyond the apex on the left side of the chest, and heard on the back near the lower angle of the scapula, denotes a regurgitant current; but a systolic murmur limited to a small area around the apex, or to the superficial cardiac space, is not proof of regurgitation. A truly regurgitant murmur, however, may be too feeble to be transmitted beyond the apex; the proof of regurgitation must then be based on other evidence associated with the murmur, namely, on enlargement of the heart and abnormal modifications of the heart-sounds.

Mitral obstruction may exist without incompetency of the mitral valve, as shown by the presence of a mitral direct, without a mitral regurgitant, murmur. The converse of this is of more frequent occurrence, that is, regurgitation may exist without obstruction. The absence, however, of a mitral direct murmur is not positive proof against mitral obstruction, for, as has been seen, the production of a characteristic mitral direct murmur, requires the obstruction to be caused by an adherence of the mitral curtains at their sides, the curtains being sufficiently flexible to vibrate with the passage of the mitral direct current of blood. Mitral obstruction and regurgitation not infrequently coexist, as shown by the presence of both the mitral direct and the mitral regurgitant murmur.

The mitral murmurs do not, *per se,* denote the amount of obstruction or regurgitation, or of both combined. Information with reference to these points may be derived from a comparison of the aortic with the pulmonic second sound. The amount of obstruction or regurgitation, or both, is great in proportion as the aortic sound is weakened. *Per contra,* there can be but little obstruction or regurgitation if the aortic and the pulmonic second sound preserve nearly or quite their normal relation to each other in respect of intensity. Information may also be obtained by analyzing the first sound as heard at the apex. In proportion as the function of the mitral valve is compromised by lesions, the valvular element of the first sound at the apex will be found deficient. In some cases the first sound in this situation has no valvular element, presenting only the characters of impulsion.

Enlargement of the right side of the heart, which results from mitral obstructive and regurgitant lesions, is a criterion of the amount of obstruction and regurgitation taken in connection with the length of time in which they have existed. Hypertrophic enlargement of the right ventricle intensifies the pulmonic second sound, and allowance must be made for this modification in determining, by a comparison of the pulmonic and the aortic sound, the degree in which the latter is weakened.

Aortic Lesions.—Lesions are localized at the aortic orifice by the aortic murmurs, namely, the aortic direct and the aortic regurgitant murmur. Aortic obstructive lesions give rise to an aortic direct murmur; but it must be considered, in the first place, that an aortic direct murmur may be inorganic, and, in the second place, that, if the murmur be organic, it may be produced by lesions which occasion no obstruction and are innocuous. The existence of obstructive lesions must be determined by evidence added to the presence of the murmur. This evidence is impairment or suppression of the aortic second sound, and enlargement of the left ventricle. If the lesions which occasion obstruction are of a character to diminish or arrest the movements of the aortic valve, the aortic second sound will be weakened or lost. If valvular lesions be limited to the aortic orifice, the degree of enlargement of the heart is a criterion of their pathological importance.

Regurgitant lesions at the aortic orifice give rise to an aortic regurgitant murmur. This murmur, of course, is always proof of regurgitation; but the murmur gives no definite information concerning the amount of incompetency of the aortic valve. A loud murmur may be produced by a regurgitant stream so small as to be, for the time, insignificant; and, on the other hand, a large regurgitant current may give rise to a feeble murmur. The extent to which the valve is damaged by the lesions, is to be determined, first, by the weakness or suppression of the aortic sound, and, second, by the degree of enlargement of the left ventricle.

Aortic obstructive and regurgitant lesions are often associated. An aortic direct and an aortic regurgitant murmur are then both present, with a weakened aortic sound or its suppression, and enlargement of the left ventricle according to the amount of the obstruction and regurgitation, together with the length of time during which the latter have existed. These effects, and not the intensity, or the pitch, or the quality of the murmurs, constitute the criterion of their pathological importance.

Mitral and aortic lesions often coexist, giving rise to two, three, or all four of the obstructive and regurgitant murmurs in the left side of the heart. In addition to the murmurs, in these cases, the effects of the combined lesions are shown in the modifications of the heart-sounds, and enlargement of both sides of the heart.

Tricuspid Lesions.—Tricuspid obstructive lesions are exceedingly rare. A few instances of the kind of obstruction which is represented by a presystolic or a tricuspid direct murmur have been reported. One instance has fallen under my observation. In this case, as in the other instances which have been reported, the tricuspid were associated with mitral lesions; hence, in localizing an obstructive lesion at the tricuspid orifice, the presence of the presystolic murmur on each side of the heart, that is, the coexistence of mitral and the tricuspid direct murmur, is to be determined. This point has already been considered (*vide* page 223).

Tricuspid regurgitation is not uncommon. Generally the insufficiency is caused by dilatation of the right ventricle occurring as an effect of mitral regurgitant or obstructive lesions. Tricuspid regurgitation is not always represented by murmur; and when a tricuspid regurgitant murmur is present, it is to be discriminated from a coexisting mitral regurgitant murmur. This point has been considered (*vide* page 224).

Pulmonic Lesions.—As compared with aortic lesions, these are of extremely infrequent occurrence, and they are generally congenital. Lesions giving rise to a pulmonic direct murmur may be localized by differentiating this murmur from the aortic direct murmur (*vide* page 224). It is to be considered that an inorganic pulmonic direct murmur is not infrequent. Pulmonic regurgitant lesions can only be diagnosticated by determining that a murmur occurring with the second sound of the heart is produced at the pulmonic and not at the aortic orifice (*vide* page 225).

Fatty Degeneration and Softening of the Heart.—Fatty degeneration of the heart is not represented by any distinctive signs; but, nevertheless, the physical diagnosis, taking into account the clinical history, may be quite positive. The signs are those which denote persistent muscular weakness of the heart. The apex-heat, if appreciable, is feeble. The intensity of the heart-sounds is diminished, and especially the intensity of the first sound. The first sound may be even suppressed over the apex, the second sound being heard in this situation. The characters of the first sound which belong to the element of impulsion are especially impaired or lost, the sound becoming short and valvular, in these respects resembling the second sound.

Now these evidences of weakened muscular power occur when the weakness is merely functional, and when the heart is enlarged by predominant dilatation. But functional weakness is generally transient, and is sufficiently explained by the existence of other than cardiac disease. Enlargement by dilatation is readily determined by physical signs. If the heart be but little or not at all enlarged, and pathological conditions adequate to explain diminished muscular power, irrespective of cardiac disease, be excluded, at the same time the signs being connected with diagnostic symptoms, the existence of fatty degeneration may be determined with much confidence.

Fatty degeneration may coexist with valvular lesions and enlargement of the heart. The physical diagnosis of fatty degeneration under these circumstances is not a simple problem. A probable diagnosis may be made when the amount of enlargement seems insufficient to account for the signs denoting muscular weakness of the heart, and when symptoms belonging to the clinical history point to fatty degeneration.

Softening of the muscular structure of the heart, occurring in continued fever and other general diseases, is denoted by the same signs which are embraced in the physical diagnosis of fatty degeneration, the most marked evidence being notable weakness, with valvular quality, or suppression, of the first sound over the apex of the heart.

Endocarditis.—The physical diagnosis of endocarditis relates almost entirely to its occurrence in connection with articular rheumatism. The diagnostic sign is a mitral systolic non-regurgitant murmur (***vide*** page 218). The presence of this murmur, however, in a case of rheumatism is not positive proof of an existing endocarditis, more especially if the patient have previously had articular rheumatism, because an endocarditis developed in a previous attack may have left a permanent murmur. If the murmur be a mitral regurgitant murmur and the heart be enlarged, it is quite certain that endocarditis has previously occurred. The positive proof is the production of the murmur during an attack of rheumatism, when previous examinations, made after the commencement of the rheumatic attack, had shown that there was no mitral murmur. An aortic direct murmur, in cases of rheumatism, is not evidence of endocarditis, because in many cases of rheumatism this murmur occurs, and is to be regarded as inorganic.

Endocarditis is probably of frequent occurrence as secondary to mitral and aortic valvular lesions; but, under these circumstances, a physical diagnosis is impracticable.

Pericarditis.—The physical diagnosis of pericarditis in the first stage, that is, prior to the effusion of liquid, is to be based on a pericardial friction murmur. Fortunately for diagnosis, this murmur is uniformly present. Its characters as contrasted with endocardial murmurs have been stated (*vide* page 227). The presence of a pericardial friction murmur, in connection with symptoms denoting pericarditis, renders the diagnosis quite positive. There is, however, one liability to error. In some cases of pleurisy or pneumonia with pleuritic inflammation, the movements of the heart occasion a rubbing of the outer surface of the pericardium against a roughened pleural surface, and in this way a cardiac pleural friction murmur is produced. This may be single or double, and when double it simulates the murmur produced within the pericardial sac. It is limited to the border of the heart, and is neither accompanied nor followed by pericardial effusion. Of course, the error of mistaking a cardiac pleural friction murmur for one produced within the pericardium, can only occur when pleurisy exists either as a primary affection or as secondary to pneumonia.

In the second stage of pericarditis, that is, after the effusion of liquid has taken place, the pericardial friction murmur often, but not always, disappears. The physical diagnosis in this stage is then to be based on the signs which show the presence of a greater or less quantity of liquid within the pericardial sac. The signs which denote pericardial effusion and its amount have been stated (*vide* page 206). With a moderate effusion, the apex of the heart is raised, and the apex-beat may be felt in the fourth intercostal space, and removed to the left of its normal situation. With considerable or large effusion, the apex-beat is lost, and the sounds of the heart are feeble and distant. The first sound loses the characters which belong to the element of impulsion, becoming short and valvular like the second sound.

Increase or diminution of liquid, in the second stage of pericarditis, is readily determined by signs obtained by percussion and auscultation. When the quantity is much diminished, the friction murmur, if it have been suppressed, returns, and persists until the pericardial surfaces become agglutinated. Not infrequently, by auscultating when the body of the patient is inclined forward, a friction murmur may be heard notwithstanding the pericardial sac contains a large quantity of liquid.

In cases of chronic pericarditis with very large effusion, dilatation of the pericardial sac is shown by signs obtained by percussion and auscultation. There is no apex impulse; the heart-sounds are feeble and distant, the first sound being short and valvular, and the præcordia may be notably projecting.

A malignant morbid growth filling the pericardial sac and inclosing within it the heart, may give rise to all the signs of pericardial effusion. A case of this kind, in a young subject, has fallen under my observation.

With reference to diagnosis, the etiological relations of pericarditis should be kept in mind. These are, acute articular rheumatism, Bright's disease, and either pleurisy or pneumonia. It rarely occurs in other connections, and, as an idiopathic affection, it is extremely rare.

The presence of air and liquid within the pericardial sac gives rise to loud splashing sounds which, occurring when respiration is suspended, and when pneumo-hydrothorax is excluded, are at once diagnostic of pneumo-hydropericardium.

Functional Disorders.—Of the varied forms of functional disorder of the heart, some are rare, and others are of frequent occurrence. A rare form is persistent frequency of the heart's action, the pulse being from 100 to 120 or more per minute, for weeks, months, and even years. This form of disorder exists in the affection known as exophthalmic goitre, Graves' or Basedow's disease. It occurs, also, without being associated with either prominence of the eyes or enlargement of the thyroid body. In a rare form the opposite of this, the action of the heart is abnormally infrequent, the pulse falling to 50, 40, 30 or less, per minute, the infrequency not being an idiosyncrasy either congenital or acquired, and continuing for a limited period. The occurrence with every alternate revolution of the heart of a ventricular systole so feeble as not to be represented by a radial pulse, is another rare form; and another is a want of synchronism in the contractions of the two ventricles, giving rise to reduplication of the heart-sounds. In the more common forms, the disorder occurs in paroxysms which are variable in duration and in the frequency of their occurrence, the heart, in the paroxysms, beating irregularly, and often with intermissions, the action in some instances being violent, and in other instances feeble or fluttering. These common forms are embraced under the name palpitation.

As regards the physical diagnosis, all the forms of disorder are in the same category; in all, the functional character of the affection is determined by exclusion, inflammatory affections and lesions being excluded by the absence of their diagnostic signs. In whatever way the action of the heart is disturbed, however great may be the disturbance, and let it be attended with ever so much distress or anxiety, if physical exploration furnish no evidence of endocarditis, pericarditis, valvular lesions, enlargement of the heart, fatty degeneration, or heart-clot, the affection is to be considered as functional. If purely functional, the affection is unattended by any danger, and is generally remediable, at least in the common forms. Hence the very great importance of a positive diagnosis.

In one point of view, the physical diagnosis in functional disorders may be said to rest, not on negative, but on positive evidence. Percussion and auscultation afford the means, not only of excluding inflammatory affections and lesions, but of demonstrating the fact that the organ is sound, at least as regards freedom from ordinary lesions. That its size is normal, is shown by the situation of the apex-beat; by ascertaining the lateral boundaries of the præcordia and the area of the superficial cardiac space. That the valves are unaffected, is shown by the normal characters of the heart-sounds. These positive facts, taken in connection with the absence of morbid signs, render the diagnosis quite certain. Moreover, the evidence, positive and negative, is readily and quickly obtained. Indeed, the time required for reaching a conclusion is so brief, that it is often politic to prolong unnecessarily the examination in order that a positive assurance of the soundness of the organ may have in the mind of the patient the weight which is desirable in order to secure relief from anxiety and apprehension.

Functional disorders are not infrequently associated with lesions with which they have no essential pathological connection. A patient with lesions which are either innocuous or attended with little, if any, inconvenience, may suffer from disturbance of the action of the heart produced by causes which are wholly independent of the lesions. There is a liability, in these cases, to the error of attributing the disorders to the lesions, and thus forming an exaggerated estimate of the importance of the latter. To decide how much of the disturbed action of the heart is due to a superadded functional affection, is not as easy as to determine that lesions do not exist. The decision must be based on the character, degree, or extent of the lesions, as evidenced by the physical signs. In this connection may be stated a practical maxim, which it is well to bear in mind, whether functional disorders exist or not, namely, valvular lesions rarely give rise to much inconvenience until they have led to enlargement of the heart; and enlargement, either with or without valvular lesions, as a rule, does not lead to the serious effects which are characteristic of cardiac disease, so long as the enlargement is due to hypertrophy and not to dilatation.

Thoracic Aneurism.

The physical conditions incident to thoracic aneurism, which are concerned in the production of signs, are, the presence of a tumor within the chest, of variable size, formed by the aneurismal sac; the passage of blood into the sac with each ventricular systole, and the expulsion of blood in the diastole by the recoil of the coats of the aneurism; the size of the opening into the sac as affecting the quantity of blood which it receives with each systole; the quantity of stratified fibrin which the sac contains; the point of connection with the aorta of the aneurismal tumor, and the direction from this point in which the tumor extends, together with its relations to the lungs, the trachea, and the primary bronchi.

With reference to diagnosis, it is well to bear in mind that, in the great majority of cases, an aortic aneurism is connected with either the ascending portion, or the junction of the ascending and the transverse portion of the arch, and that the tumor generally extends to the right in a lateral or anterolateral direction. The physical diagnosis is more easily made when the aneurismal tumor is thus connected. The signs are less available if the aneurism arise from the transverse or descending aorta, and especially if the tumor extends in a direction downward or backward.

An aneurismal tumor which has made its way through the walls of the chest, or which, without perforation, causes a circumscribed bulging, obvious to the eye and touch, presents the following diagnostic signs: An impulse is seen and felt which is synchronous with the ventricular systole. The force of the impulse is variable, depending, aside from the force with which the left ventricle contracts, upon the size of the orifice between the sac and the artery, and the quantity of fibrin which the sac contains. A vibration or thrill with each impulse is sometimes a marked sign, but is often wanting. Frequently, but by no means constantly, a systolic murmur is heard over the tumor, and there may be also a diastolic murmur produced by the passage of blood from the sac. The heart-sounds over the tumor are more or less intense. There is notable dulness on percussion over an area corresponding to the space within the chest which the tumor occupies. If the tumor be of considerable size, it may produce condensation of lung around it; the area of dulness on percussion will be in this way extended beyond the limits of the tumor. Under these circumstances, bronchial respiration and bronchophony may be produced. If the aneurismal sac be beneath the integument, there may be to the touch a sense of fluctuation.

With the foregoing signs, the physical diagnosis scarcely admits of doubt. Some of the signs may be produced by a tumor, not aneurismal, which is so situated as to receive and conduct the aortic impulse. The chances of a tumor being so situated as to simulate the signs of an aneurism are very few. I have met with a case of empyema in which perforation of the chest took place in the second intercostal space on the right side of the sternum, giving rise in this situation to a fluctuating tumor which had a strong pulsation. On a superficial examination the case seemed clearly one of aneurism: but an examination of the chest showed the right pleural cavity to be filled with liquid, and a puncture in the axillary region gave exit to a large quantity of pus, the pulsating tumor disappearing after a certain quantity of the purulent liquid had escaped.

When, from its small size or its situation, an aneurismal tumor does not come into contact with the thoracic wall, and when it is situated beneath the sternum, signs obtained by palpation and inspection being absent, the physical diagnosis is less easy. Important signs are, dulness within a circumscribed space situated in the course of the aorta; an abnormal transmission of the heart-sounds within this space, and the presence of murmurs. These signs are not always available, and when present they are not sufficient for a positive diagnosis. Other physical evidence and the presence of certain symptoms render the existence of aneurism highly probable either with or without the foregoing signs. If an aneurismal tumor press upon the trachea, it occasions a tracheal sound, or stridor, together with weakness of the respiratory murmur on both sides of the chest. If the tumor press upon a primary bronchus, it occasions diminished or suppressed respiratory murmur on one side, and increased respiratory murmur on the other side of the chest. These physical signs should always lead to a suspicion of aneurism in a person forty years of age. Symptoms which should excite this suspicion and lead to careful physical explora-

www.bookjungle.com *email: sales@bookjungle.com fax: 630-214-0564 mail: Book Jungle PO Box 2226 Champaign, IL 61825*

The Codes Of Hammurabi And Moses
W. W. Davies

QTY

The discovery of the Hammurabi Code is one of the greatest achievements of archaeology, and is of paramount interest, not only to the student of the Bible, but also to all those interested in ancient history...

Religion   **ISBN:** *1-59462-338-4*   Pages:132
   MSRP $12.95

The Theory of Moral Sentiments
Adam Smith

QTY

This work from 1749. contains original theories of conscience amd moral judgment and it is the foundation for systemof morals.

Philosophy   **ISBN:** *1-59462-777-0*   Pages:536
   MSRP $19.95

Jessica's First Prayer
Hesba Stretton

QTY

In a screened and secluded corner of one of the many railway-bridges which span the streets of London there could be seen a few years ago, from five o'clock every morning until half past eight, a tidily set-out coffee-stall, consisting of a trestle and board, upon which stood two large tin cans, with a small fire of charcoal burning under each so as to keep the coffee boiling during the early hours of the morning when the work-people were thronging into the city on their way to their daily toil...

Childrens   **ISBN:** *1-59462-373-2*   Pages:84
   MSRP $9.95

My Life and Work
Henry Ford

QTY

Henry Ford revolutionized the world with his implementation of mass production for the Model T automobile. Gain valuable business insight into his life and work with his own auto-biography... "We have only started on our development of our country we have not as yet, with all our talk of wonderful progress, done more than scratch the surface. The progress has been wonderful enough but..."

Biographies/   **ISBN:** *1-59462-198-5*   Pages:300
   MSRP $21.95

www.bookjungle.com *email: sales@bookjungle.com fax: 630-214-0564 mail: Book Jungle PO Box 2226 Champaign, IL 61825*

The Art of Cross-Examination
Francis Wellman

QTY

I presume it is the experience of every author, after his first book is published upon an important subject, to be almost overwhelmed with a wealth of ideas and illustrations which could readily have been included in his book, and which to his own mind, at least, seem to make a second edition inevitable. Such certainly was the case with me; and when the first edition had reached its sixth impression in five months, I rejoiced to learn that it seemed to my publishers that the book had met with a sufficiently favorable reception to justify a second and considerably enlarged edition. ...

Reference   ISBN: *1-59462-647-2*   Pages:412 MSRP *$19.95*

On the Duty of Civil Disobedience
Henry David Thoreau

QTY

Thoreau wrote his famous essay, On the Duty of Civil Disobedience, as a protest against an unjust but popular war and the immoral but popular institution of slave-owning. He did more than write—he declined to pay his taxes, and was hauled off to gaol in consequence. Who can say how much this refusal of his hastened the end of the war and of slavery ?

Law   ISBN: *1-59462-747-9*   Pages:48 MSRP *$7.45*

Dream Psychology Psychoanalysis for Beginners
Sigmund Freud

QTY

Sigmund Freud, born Sigismund Schlomo Freud (May 6, 1856 - September 23, 1939), was a Jewish-Austrian neurologist and psychiatrist who co-founded the psychoanalytic school of psychology. Freud is best known for his theories of the unconscious mind, especially involving the mechanism of repression; his redefinition of sexual desire as mobile and directed towards a wide variety of objects; and his therapeutic techniques, especially his understanding of transference in the therapeutic relationship and the presumed value of dreams as sources of insight into unconscious desires.

Psychology   ISBN: *1-59462-905-6*   Pages:196 MSRP *$15.45*

The Miracle of Right Thought
Orison Swett Marden

QTY

Believe with all of your heart that you will do what you were made to do. When the mind has once formed the habit of holding cheerful, happy, prosperous pictures, it will not be easy to form the opposite habit. It does not matter how improbable or how far away this realization may see, or how dark the prospects may be, if we visualize them as best we can, as vividly as possible, hold tenaciously to them and vigorously struggle to attain them, they will gradually become actualized, realized in the life. But a desire, a longing without endeavor, a yearning abandoned or held indifferently will vanish without realization.

Self Help   ISBN: *1-59462-644-8*   Pages:360 MSRP *$25.45*

www.bookjungle.com *email: sales@bookjungle.com fax: 630-214-0564 mail: Book Jungle PO Box 2226 Champaign, IL 61825*

QTY

| | **The Rosicrucian Cosmo-Conception Mystic Christianity** by *Max Heindel* | ISBN: *1-59462-188-8* | **$38.95** |

The Rosicrucian Cosmo-conception is not dogmatic, neither does it appeal to any other authority than the reason of the student. It is: not controversial, but is: sent forth in the, hope that it may help to clear... — New Age/Religion Pages 646

Abandonment To Divine Providence by *Jean-Pierre de Caussade*   ISBN: *1-59462-228-0*   **$25.95**
"The Rev. Jean Pierre de Caussade was one of the most remarkable spiritual writers of the Society of Jesus in France in the 18th Century. His death took place at Toulouse in 1751. His works have gone through many editions and have been republished..." — Inspirational/Religion Pages 400

Mental Chemistry by *Charles Haanel*   ISBN: *1-59462-192-6*   **$23.95**
Mental Chemistry allows the change of material conditions by combining and appropriately utilizing the power of the mind. Much like applied chemistry creates something new and unique out of careful combinations of chemicals the mastery of mental chemistry... — New Age Pages 354

The Letters of Robert Browning and Elizabeth Barret Barrett 1845-1846 vol II   ISBN: *1-59462-193-4*   **$35.95**
by *Robert Browning* and *Elizabeth Barrett* — Biographies Pages 596

Gleanings In Genesis (volume I) by *Arthur W. Pink*   ISBN: *1-59462-130-6*   **$27.45**
Appropriately has Genesis been termed "the seed plot of the Bible" for in it we have, in germ form, almost all of the great doctrines which are afterwards fully developed in the books of Scripture which follow... — Religion/Inspirational Pages 420

The Master Key by *L. W. de Laurence*   ISBN: *1-59462-001-6*   **$30.95**
In no branch of human knowledge has there been a more lively increase of the spirit of research during the past few years than in the study of Psychology, Concentration and Mental Discipline. The requests for authentic lessons in Thought Control, Mental Discipline and... — New Age/Business Pages 422

The Lesser Key Of Solomon Goetia by *L. W. de Laurence*   ISBN: *1-59462-092-X*   **$9.95**
This translation of the first book of the "Lemegton" which is now for the first time made accessible to students of Talismanic Magic was done, after careful collation and edition, from numerous Ancient Manuscripts in Hebrew, Latin, and French... — New Age/Occult Pages 92

Rubaiyat Of Omar Khayyam by *Edward Fitzgerald*   ISBN: *1-59462-332-5*   **$13.95**
Edward Fitzgerald, whom the world has already learned, in spite of his own efforts to remain within the shadow of anonymity, to look upon as one of the rarest poets of the century, was born at Bredfield, in Suffolk, on the 31st of March, 1809. He was the third son of John Purcell... — Music Pages 172

Ancient Law by *Henry Maine*   ISBN: *1-59462-128-4*   **$29.95**
The chief object of the following pages is to indicate some of the earliest ideas of mankind, as they are reflected in Ancient Law, and to point out the relation of those ideas to modern thought. — Religion/History Pages 452

Far-Away Stories by *William J. Locke*   ISBN: *1-59462-129-2*   **$19.45**
"Good wine needs no bush, but a collection of mixed vintages does. And this book is just such a collection. Some of the stories I do not want to remain buried for ever in the museum files of dead magazine-numbers an author's not unpardonable vanity..." — Fiction Pages 272

Life of David Crockett by *David Crockett*   ISBN: *1-59462-250-7*   **$27.45**
"Colonel David Crockett was one of the most remarkable men of the times in which he lived. Born in humble life, but gifted with a strong will, an indomitable courage, and unremitting perseverance... — Biographies/New Age Pages 424

Lip-Reading by *Edward Nitchie*   ISBN: *1-59462-206-X*   **$25.95**
Edward B. Nitchie, founder of the New York School for the Hard of Hearing, now the Nitchie School of Lip-Reading, Inc, wrote "LIP-READING Principles and Practice". The development and perfecting of this meritorious work on lip-reading was an undertaking... — How-to Pages 400

A Handbook of Suggestive Therapeutics, Applied Hypnotism, Psychic Science   ISBN: *1-59462-214-0*   **$24.95**
by *Henry Munro* — Health/New Age/Health/Self-help Pages 376

A Doll's House: and Two Other Plays by *Henrik Ibsen*   ISBN: *1-59462-112-8*   **$19.95**
Henrik Ibsen created this classic when in revolutionary 1848 Rome. Introducing some striking concepts in playwriting for the realist genre, this play has been studied the world over. — Fiction/Classics/Plays 308

The Light of Asia by *sir Edwin Arnold*   ISBN: *1-59462-204-3*   **$13.95**
In this poetic masterpiece, Edwin Arnold describes the life and teachings of Buddha. The man who was to become known as Buddha to the world was born as Prince Gautama of India but he rejected the worldly riches and abandoned the reigns of power when... — Religion/History/Biographies Pages 170

The Complete Works of Guy de Maupassant by *Guy de Maupassant*   ISBN: *1-59462-157-8*   **$16.95**
"For days and days, nights and nights, I had dreamed of that first kiss which was to consecrate our engagement, and I knew not on what spot I should put my lips..." — Fiction/Classics Pages 240

The Art of Cross-Examination by *Francis L. Wellman*   ISBN: *1-59462-309-0*   **$26.95**
Written by a renowned trial lawyer, Wellman imparts his experience and uses case studies to explain how to use psychology to extract desired information through questioning. — How-to/Science/Reference Pages 408

Answered or Unanswered? by *Louisa Vaughan*   ISBN: *1-59462-248-5*   **$10.95**
Miracles of Faith in China — Religion Pages 112

The Edinburgh Lectures on Mental Science (1909) by *Thomas*   ISBN: *1-59462-008-3*   **$11.95**
This book contains the substance of a course of lectures recently given by the writer in the Queen Street Hall, Edinburgh. Its purpose is to indicate the Natural Principles governing the relation between Mental Action and Material Conditions... — New Age/Psychology Pages 148

Ayesha by *H. Rider Haggard*   ISBN: *1-59462-301-5*   **$24.95**
Verily and indeed it is the unexpected that happens! Probably if there was one person upon the earth from whom the Editor of this, and of a certain previous history, did not expect to hear again... — Classics Pages 380

Ayala's Angel by *Anthony Trollope*   ISBN: *1-59462-352-X*   **$29.95**
The two girls were both pretty, but Lucy who was twenty-one who supposed to be simple and comparatively unattractive, whereas Ayala was credited, as her Bombwhat romantic name might show, with poetic charm and a taste for romance. Ayala when her father died was nineteen... — Fiction Pages 484

The American Commonwealth by *James Bryce*   ISBN: *1-59462-286-8*   **$34.45**
An interpretation of American democratic political theory. It examines political mechanics and society from the perspective of Scotsman James Bryce — Politics Pages 572

Stories of the Pilgrims by *Margaret P. Pumphrey*   ISBN: *1-59462-116-0*   **$17.95**
This book explores pilgrims religious oppression in England as well as their escape to Holland and eventual crossing to America on the Mayflower, and their early days in New England... — History Pages 268

www.bookjungle.com email: sales@bookjungle.com fax: 630-214-0564 mail: Book Jungle PO Box 2226 Champaign, IL 61825

			QTY
The Fasting Cure by *Sinclair Upton*	ISBN: *1-59462-222-1*	**$13.95**	☐
In the Cosmopolitan Magazine for May, 1910, and in the Contemporary Review (London) for April, 1910, I published an article dealing with my experiences in fasting. I have written a great many magazine articles, but never one which attracted so much attention... New Age/Self Help/Health Pages 164			
Hebrew Astrology by *Sepharial*	ISBN: *1-59462-308-2*	**$13.45**	☐
In these days of advanced thinking it is a matter of common observation that we have left many of the old landmarks behind and that we are now pressing forward to greater heights and to a wider horizon than that which represented the mind-content of our progenitors... Astrology Pages 144			
Thought Vibration or The Law of Attraction in the Thought World	ISBN: *1-59462-127-6*	**$12.95**	☐
by *William Walker Atkinson*	Psychology/Religion Pages 144		
Optimism by *Helen Keller*	ISBN: *1-59462-108-X*	**$15.95**	☐
Helen Keller was blind, deaf, and mute since 19 months old, yet famously learned how to overcome these handicaps, communicate with the world, and spread her lectures promoting optimism. An inspiring read for everyone... Biographies/Inspirational Pages 84			
Sara Crewe by *Frances Burnett*	ISBN: *1-59462-360-0*	**$9.45**	☐
In the first place, Miss Minchin lived in London. Her home was a large, dull, tall one, in a large, dull square, where all the houses were alike, and all the sparrows were alike, and where all the door-knockers made the same heavy sound... Childrens/Classic Pages 88			
The Autobiography of Benjamin Franklin by *Benjamin Franklin*	ISBN: *1-59462-135-7*	**$24.95**	☐
The Autobiography of Benjamin Franklin has probably been more extensively read than any other American historical work, and no other book of its kind has had such ups and downs of fortune. Franklin lived for many years in England, where he was agent... Biographies/History Pages 332			

Name	
Email	
Telephone	
Address	
City, State ZIP	

☐ Credit Card   ☐ Check / Money Order

Credit Card Number	
Expiration Date	
Signature	

Please Mail to: Book Jungle
                 PO Box 2226
                 Champaign, IL 61825
or Fax to: 630-214-0564

ORDERING INFORMATION

web: *www.bookjungle.com*
email: *sales@bookjungle.com*
fax: *630-214-0564*
mail: *Book Jungle PO Box 2226 Champaign, IL 61825*
or PayPal *to sales@bookjungle.com*

Please contact us for bulk discounts

DIRECT-ORDER TERMS

**20% Discount if You Order
Two or More Books**
Free Domestic Shipping!
Accepted: Master Card, Visa,
Discover, American Express